Create Your Freedom:

Become a Local Web Design Guru and Make Money from Home

By Ray DelVecchio

Text copyright © 2015 Ray DelVecchio

All Rights Reserved

Table of Contents

Preface... 1

Chapter 1 - My Story.. 3

    Growing Up... 3

    High School... 5

    College... 6

    Graduate School.. 8

    Starting a Business... 12

Chapter 2 - Web Design History...................................... 14

    1990s.. 14

    2000s.. 16

    2010s.. 18

Chapter 3 - Future Trends.. 19

    The World is Going Mobile.. 19

    The Rise of Website Generators............................... 20

    The Rise of the Personal Brand................................ 21

Chapter 4 - Identify Your Best Skills.............................. 23

    This is Not a Career Move... 23

    What Can You Learn Through a Website?............. 26

    Connect the Dots.. 27

Chapter 5 - Pick a Platform and Master It 30

Why Use WordPress.org 30

Why is WordPress So Popular? 30

Utilize Your Strengths 32

When NOT to Use WordPress.org 34

Chapter 6 - Fundamentals of Business 37

Increase Cash Flow 38

You are the Salesperson 39

Think Like the Customer 40

Solve Their Problem 41

Reinvest in Yourself 43

Freelancer vs. Business Owner 45

Chapter 7 - Getting Your First Client 48

TIP #1: Get Attention 48

TIP #2: Use Your Personal Network 49

TIP #3: Go the Extra Mile (And Be Memorable) ... 51

TIP #4: Sell Results, Not Features 53

Chapter 8 - Pricing Structures and Payments 55

Cheap Prices = Cheap Customers 57

Client Questionnaire 58

Determining the Project Cost 61

Other Pricing Structures 64

Accepting Payments 65

When to Avoid a Formal Contract 66

Chapter 9 - Web Design Process 69

Domain & Web Hosting 70

Installing WordPress 73

Finding Relevant Examples 73

Choosing a Premium Theme 75

Building the Layout 76

Adding Pages 76

Adding Plugins 78

Getting Ready to Launch 84

Monitoring Post-Launch 85

Repurpose From Project to Project 90

Chapter 10 - Client & Project Management 92

Organize Your Life 92

Utilize Cloud Services 102

Take the Reigns 105

Chapter 11 - Get Found on Google 107

v

- Method #1 - Pay for Instant Traffic.................................109
- Method #2 - SEO + Content Marketing........................110

Chapter 12 - Build Your Systems..121
- Financial.. 121
- Marketing... 122
- Sales.. 124
- Training.. 125

Chapter 13 - Expanding and Growing......................................127
- Upsell Your Current Clients... 128
- Ask For Referrals.. 129
- Creative Google Search... 129
- Blog Your Experiences.. 132
- Sell Previous Results.. 133
- Outsource or Partner.. 134

Get Started Today... 137

List of Resources.. 139
- Books.. 139
- Business... 141
- Color Scheme.. 141
- Copywriting... 141

CSS 142

Domain Registration 142

Fonts 142

Google Chrome Browser Add-Ons 143

HTML 143

Images 144

jQuery 144

Measurement & Tracking 144

Productivity & Efficiency 145

Q/A + Forums 145

SEO 145

Social Media & Sharing 146

Testing Tools 146

Textures & Patterns 147

Vectors & Graphics 147

Website Hosting 147

WordPress 147

WordPress Plugins – My Favorites 148

Preface

Can a 1-page site be worth $1,000,000?

It doesn't sound realistic. However in 2005, that was Alex Tew's goal by creating a 1-page website with a 1,000 x 1,000 pixel grid for banner advertising. It was called "The Million Dollar Homepage" - anyone was allowed to purchase ad space for $1 per pixel.

Within the first 5 months he surpassed $1M in gross sales, fueled by publicity on major news sources.

I tried my hand at a few of these money focused projects. Unless you are lucky, they will fail. You must be driven by something other than financial success to push through roadblocks.

The news isn't all bad, though, because I know you can make good money with websites.

Are you passionate about the web? Do you want to use those skills to supplement your income? Or do you have dreams of starting your own business someday?

There has never been a better time than today to get up to speed with websites, online marketing, and the digital world.

Having a website is the key to connecting people online, whether it's your local community or around the globe. And it's really easy to set one up with WordPress.

The most reliable way to make your first dollar is by managing the websites of local businesses. Many of them are a one-man or woman operation working from home. If not, less than 5 full-time employees is typical.

The best clients are successful offline, and they have both the willingness and ability to pay what you're worth to implement online strategies.

Your advantage is the personal touch, whether it's meeting in person or connecting through Skype or Facetime. The goal is to learn from each other and build long-term trust.

The journey can be bumpy. Don't forget that even if your situation is tough, you're learning something valuable that will affect you for the rest of your life. It's going to make you wiser in all future situations.

The future of the web will be a fun ride. Get onboard and take advantage of all the amazing resources available today that allow us to do meaningful work and create more freedom in our lives!

Chapter 1 - My Story

Hello there, I'm Ray DelVecchio. First - thank you for reading!

If one person takes action and learns something new, this book was worthwhile.

Working with websites is fun, and it's an ideal way to learn business skills without a major financial investment.

The potential rewards are limitless if you are dedicated to investing in yourself and continuously improving.

You can make money with products (directly/drop-shipping), services (web/graphic design), education (e-books/courses), or "sell" space on your website (banner ads/affiliate offers).

I've dabbled with all of them, and have enjoyed the most success from managing the online presence of local clients.

Not only can you make quick money by selling your services, but you also build real relationships since you meet with your clients in person.

Now, I want to share what I've learned over the years.

Growing Up

Being born in the mid 1980's, I had a computer available to me for my entire life. I distinctly remember using floppy disks and the MS-DOS operating system at my first home PC.

At elementary school, play-time alternated between kickball outside and games on the classroom computer.

These were classics like "The Oregon Trail" and "Where in the World is Carmen Sandiego".

And I was a prototypical good student ever since preschool – following directions, taking notes and memorizing was easy for me.

I didn't think much of this until 5th grade, when my teacher proclaimed that I was one of the best students in her class during a private parent-teacher conference.

It was a proud moment.

But in retrospect, I was really driven by being good at school. That was my competition. I didn't have a vision or specific passion for my future and career.

To illustrate this point, when I was younger I aspired to be a garbage man.

Don't ask me why, I was fascinated by them when they picked up the trash each week. Probably because of the truck.

As you can tell, my bar was set pretty low from the beginning.

High School

This was the beginning of the Google era.

In 9th grade Biology, we had to research and write a report on an animal.

I chose the African Lion.

At the time, there were a handful of search engines like AltaVista and Ask Jeeves. Our teacher, Mr. Peterson, was a smart man. He said, "use Google, it's WAY better".

He was right. That was the moment I first became sold on the power of Google.

It was amazing that you could find almost anything you wanted to know, on any subject, in a matter of minutes.

From that point on, I really took off at school. I cannot tell you how many times people asked me, "how do you know about that?" or "how did you do so well on that?".

Simple - I was curious or obligated to complete an assignment and I searched Google. Then I found the info and read it. That's it.

Even though I never considered myself astute with business, I did have a brief moment of entrepreneurship.

I used Napster and other file sharing software to download music, then burn custom CDs for $5 each.

People would give me a list of songs they wanted on paper, and I'd find them, download them, and produce

5

their favorite mix. Being a perfectionist, I even included a hard-case insert with a printed list of songs.

I didn't make a killing, yet simply making a few extra bucks because of my computer skills was a great feeling.

That feeling stuck with me, that my knowledge could be turned into money. But I didn't really understand how to act on it.

To me, success meant going to school, getting a degree and finding a job. I was blind to alternate paths.

I ultimately finished 2nd in my high school graduating class, and went on to college for computer & electrical engineering. I chose between that and computer science.

But I thought engineering would give me a deeper perspective of technology.

College

I look at the 4 years of college like a sandwich.

Freshman and senior year had moments of difficulty, but overall were doable.

Sophomore and junior years were pure torture. Pardon my french, some of our professors were real assholes. Others were brilliant minds and great mentors, so that was the give and take.

I didn't have much of a life those two years. I was routinely going to classes early in the morning, staying in the lab until late afternoon, doing homework and studying until 3AM, going to bed and getting 3-4 hours sleep. Some nights less, rarely more.

This cycle repeated again and again.

For the majority of the year, it was 5-6 days a week. For the last couple weeks of the semester, it was like that 7 days a week. I honestly don't think I had a full Saturday and Sunday those years without at least 2-3 hours of work sprinkled in.

Several of my classmates would sleep in the lab because it was easier. They would get pizza delivered to the engineering building and fuel themselves with Monster energy drinks.

Sleeping in my own bed was a high priority. However, compared to my friends who were business and communication majors, I didn't have much time to unwind.

I was hell-bent on doing well. I hated getting C's or D's on anything. That, to me, meant failure.

And with a lot of elbow grease and stress, I graduated near the top of my engineering class.

Our professor sat us all down one day and asked, "How many of you have jobs lined up?" About half of the students raised their hands, myself excluded.

He then asked, "How many are going to grad school?" Another quarter raised their hands, myself excluded again.

He finished with, "Why aren't the rest of you? It's free learning if you get a stipend and you'll earn more at your first job".

So I prepared multiple applications for a Master's degree, got accepted to each university, and chose the one that covered all my costs.

Graduate School

The tuition was paid for and the stipend covered my rent and food, so I won't complain.

Plus my advisor, Dr. K, was possibly the coolest guy in the engineering department.

Even though I wasn't the ideal graduate student, he did show me how to lead a group of people where the direction was determined by everyone's interests.

He didn't run a dictatorship, you were free to explore. That's how you achieve peak productivity.

The co-leader, Nick, was the smartest person I've ever met. You could ask him about anything, from 15th century history to South Korean culture to integrated circuit design to programming languages. It didn't matter, he would have a completely logical answer and viewpoint.

The lab group was referred to as a "pirate ship". Computer hacking, security, and hardware design were the principle interests. Our rooms were messy with wires and testing tools. Breaking things was not only acceptable, but encouraged.

We even went to the DEFCON hacking conference in Las Vegas to present our work.

Overall, I thought the entire atmosphere of the group was unique. And that was 100% fostered by my advisor.

Unfortunately, I didn't contribute as much as I probably could have.

In the latter part of my college years I was slowly realizing a huge problem. I was not passionate at all about what I was doing. It was work that began to interest me less and less. Going into the lab felt like a duty rather than enjoyable.

You might ask yourself, why the heck did you get your Master's degree?!?

Great question. And my current 29-year old self would say I was a masochist.

The truth is that I didn't have any idea what kind of career I wanted. So instead of doing something for myself, I listened to my undergraduate professor.

Not the best decision in hindsight.

Fast forward after I finished my Master's thesis (which was delayed due to a crashed hard drive), and I was experiencing serious burnout.

I made a decision that shocked my friends and family, and opted against committing to a $75,000/year job that would have set me up for life. I essentially did nothing, moved back to my parents house, and chose to take my time.

It was a moment of my life that would have delighted Peter Gibbons from "Office Space". And it wasn't an easy decision, but my motives went beyond money.

It came down to time and the 30+ year commitment I would have been making by entering the workforce.

Here's the actual list that I considered:

Money - There is no argument here. After working at a Lone Star Steakhouse, CVS Pharmacy and a physically demanding job as a mover one summer, I could live quite comfortably with a computer engineer's yearly income.

Time - My weeks would consist of 40-60 hours in an office or traveling, plus 1-2 weeks of vacation a year. 8AM every morning, non-negotiable in most cases. Not appealing since I was a night owl in my early 20's. Not to mention that you still are trading your time for dollars, albeit at a higher rate. Still, long-term financial leverage isn't there with a salary-based income. If I work 2x as hard, I don't get paid double.

Commitment - In theory, you can switch jobs at any point. In reality, when you become comfortable making over $50,000/year, it's difficult to ditch that for any personal dream, however big. And I have a lot of things

I'd like to accomplish in life other than sit in a cubicle or office working on someone else's ideas.

Mental Effort - Engineering is brutal. I can tell you that first hand. Don't get me wrong, I LOVE technology. But during my days at school, it became apparent that everyone around me lit up while talking about their microchip and artificial-intelligence projects. Meanwhile, I was struggling to put in enough hours to adequately communicate with these brilliant people. Staying current with engineering trends would have sapped every ounce of my brain power and creative energy.

Passion - This was the overall deciding factor. I wasn't cut out for engineering and it took me 6 years of college to figure it out. For a period, I was convinced that I was an idiot. It turns out millions experience that same feeling of indecisiveness during or after college. Don't worry if it's you, there is plenty of time ahead!

I'm not saying college is wrong for everyone.

However, we are collectively seeing too many people pay $100,000+ to forget 95% of what they learn, and no closer to finding work that truly inspires them.

Meanwhile, better resources for learning are popping up everyday on the internet.

My mindset is this - why not invest a small fraction of what you paid for college into something you really love? If you do that, the knowledge will compound immensely in a much shorter timeframe.

My goal for this book is for you to get a lot more value than the cost (<$10).

Starting a Business

There was a huge unknown in front of me, and it was finally exciting. Don't be fooled, I was nervous, too.

I started my quest learning about websites as a hobby in the years prior. And I chose to set up an NFL Sports Blog on WordPress as my first project. This was my way to learn what it took to create a large website from scratch.

Plus I thought it would turn into the next big thing by getting listed on Google and the money would come pouring in. Ah, the wide-eyed days.

At this time I had no clients and no income. Zilch, zero.

However, I was thoroughly enjoying every moment of the process and was learning at a torrid pace. Even being next to broke, and with some admonishment by friends, my vision was finally clear.

There were nights I worked until 4AM fixing bugs on the NFL website, and I would get up 7 hours later then continue within 10 minutes of being awake after brushing my teeth.

Two major takeaways:

Get 7-8 Hours Sleep - Your body needs it to get in a rhythm and create the momentum you need. I realize this may not always be possible, i.e. if you have kids. But do your best to rest while you can. Not just physically but mentally. You need a clear mind to be effective.

Time Flies When You Have Fun - If you enjoy something, time can fly. It's being in a state of flow or as athletes say, "the zone". You are invigorated to uncover the next step and improve. When you learn something new it's intriguing and not daunting (well maybe a little). You realize that the end goal is far away but you can see the small steps it takes to get there and you put your head down to do the work.

I was hustling for a few bucks with my computer skills and graciously accepting free home-cooked meals as often as possible (my mom is the best). If you have that type of support, utilize it to the fullest extent so you don't bury yourself in debt!

Within a couple months, I got my first two paying website customers through my personal network. To this day, those initial customers still pay me monthly.

Through referrals I found broader opportunities. When more and more folks knew that I could do a variety of cool stuff with websites and computers, they started finding me.

The barrier to entry to starting your business is much greater in your mind than in reality.

It doesn't take 4 years of college to learn web design or online marketing. It takes persistence, determination and most importantly a desire to actually help the people that pay for your services!

Chapter 2 - Web Design History

Web design, to me, is simply the act of putting together a website.

It's one of several titles that can be ambiguous, i.e. web designer, web developer, webmaster.

Today, you don't have to be a designer nor a tech genius to build a great looking website for you or a business that pays you.

That wasn't always the case.

1990s

In the early part of this decade, the internet largely consisted of text based sites, the first one created by Tim Berners-Lee, a CERN (European Organization for Nuclear Research) computer scientist.

CERN is better known today for the Large Hadron Collider (LHC), the most powerful particle accelerator in the world.

Once websites became widespread, the Word Wide Web Consortium (W3C) was formed in 1994 by Tim Berners-Lee to develop standards to increase compatibility across browsers and devices.

Below is an example of an early website:

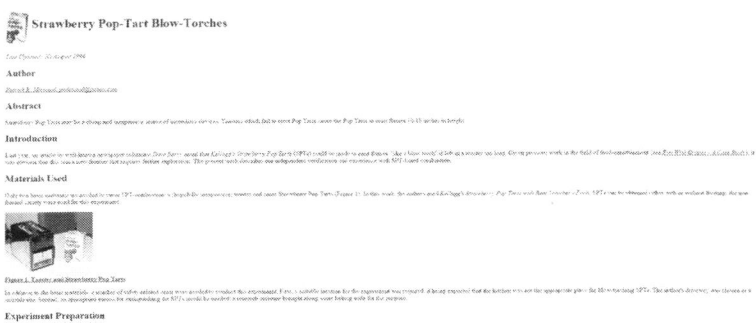

Around 1995, the plain website layout evolved by using table-based designs. This allowed multi-column websites and it created a better model for navigation and organization.

Several online page builders emerged, which allowed anyone to create a web page about themselves or their interests. Some examples include GeoCities and AngelFire.

Check out this example (which still works) from the movie Space Jam:

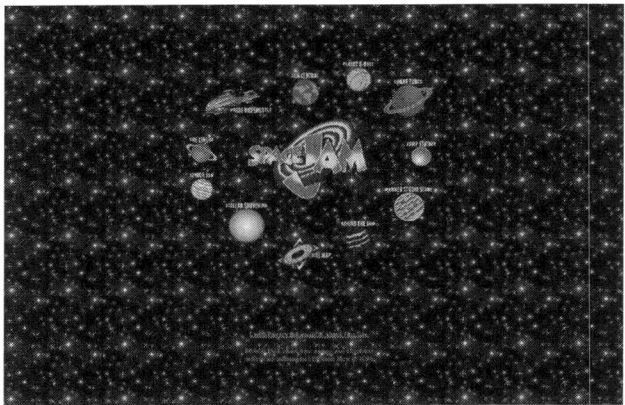

15

In the late 1990s, the web became more dynamic. This was accomplished with two technologies that gained popularity - Adobe Flash and PHP.

For business and entertainment websites, it was common to see a table-based design, with a handful of Adobe Flash elements to make the website interactive.

This was also the era of "splash pages", where you are greeted by an animation and need to click "enter" to get to the homepage. Not a great technique for user experience, but people love to show off features of the latest technology!

2000s

In 2000, Cascading Style Sheets (CSS) really began to take off.

If you are unfamiliar with CSS, it's what separates the design of the webpage from the content. You can have the same HTML/text/images on a page, but two completely different looks if you make enough changes to the CSS files.

Travel back in time to this MySpace bulletin from "Tom":

This is also the decade when more interactivity was developed into websites using Javascript.

Adobe Flash, once a big part of the web, declined in popularity due to device compatibility and SEO issues.

To be more specific, Adobe Flash was often used to create an interactive navigation bar. The problem is Google had trouble identifying any content within a Flash module (SWF file extension).

Several pages on these websites were not being indexed on Google as a result.

If you used this design strategy, you would lose out on Google as a traffic source because they wouldn't rank you for any of your desired keywords. And that's a big no-no for marketing a website post-launch.

My absolute favorite website software - WordPress - was originally released in 2003. It started as a blogging tool, but developed into the most popular content management system on the internet.

More on that later...

17

2010s

Interactivity is taken to a new level with the development of web apps using Asynchronous Javascript and XML (AJAX).

With the rise of the iPhone and other smart devices, mobile web design became a hot trend for a couple years.

However, people soon realized that it was impossible to design a separate website for every device that would come out in the future. Smartphones, tablets and e-readers came in all different sizes, it was too much.

That was the seed that blossomed into responsive web design.

Today, using CSS media queries, you can make your website responsive by adjusting the layout at any pixel width. And once these settings are in place, it does this on the fly when you change the width of your browser window.

So what does the future hold?

Chapter 3 - Future Trends

If there is one thing I know, it's that you cannot predict the future. No one can.

What you can do is spot trends and become an early adopter. The more you ride the wave and understand new technologies, the better off you will be.

Here are some trends we cannot ignore.

The World is Going Mobile

"Power users" still use desktops. And they will for the foreseeable future.

But the average person uses what is most convenient for them.

That is their phone or tablet nowadays.

Don't take my word, let me review the website data from a client of mine. I've managed his residential services website for the past 4 years, and these are the trends across 15,000+ local visitors:

- **2011** - 89% Desktop / 9% Mobile / 2% Tablet
- **2012** - 86% Desktop / 9% Mobile / 5% Tablet
- **2013** - 75% Desktop / 14% Mobile / 11% Tablet
- **2014** - 62% Desktop / 25% Mobile / 13% Tablet

It doesn't take too much thinking to realize that in 2015, mobile and tablets will continue to cut into the desktop total.

The Rise of Website Generators

We are being inundated with simple options to create a website.

Off the top of my head, I'll name a few that start with a low monthly cost: Squarespace, Wix, Weebly, Web.com, GoDaddy, VistaPrint, YellowPages, Network Solutions, Homestead, SuperMedia, 1and1, HIBU.

It can be intimidating.

Trust me when I say that there are plenty of business owners and other folks who need a website but don't want to do-it-themselves. Technology moves a lot faster than people.

My advice?

Ignore the noise, and learn a powerful content management system like WordPress to develop your own skills. Both with websites and business.

Because of the fierce competition, I don't think your goal should be to create a $10 million web design agency. It's possible, but think smaller because the big guys are taking over that high-volume market.

It's totally within reach to find 2-3 great clients that will set you up to explore your curiosity, expand your creativity, and create your own path.

All while making cash on the side to build momentum.

The Rise of the Personal Brand

I come across more websites now than ever before, where people are creating content they love, and building an engaged audience through the distribution of social media and paid advertisements.

This is exactly what I'm doing with this book. I love websites, I love WordPress, I love online marketing, and I want to share my experiences with as many like-minded people as possible.

One of my favorite writers and entrepreneurs is James Altucher. He is a board member of a staffing agency with $1 billion dollars in revenue.

In his books, he discusses how the future is trending in every sector towards less full-time employees, and more outsourcing and temp jobs. This can be frightening to most people, because they equate personal security to having a job.

I did for 22 years of my life, until I realized it was time to get one.

He goes on to eloquently describe the current marketplace on the web.

Is it crowded? Of course. Yet the barrier to entry to build a side-income or full-time business is lower than ever because of free technology resources available to us.

He always reinforces, "the gatekeepers to your success are going away". To clarify what that means, ask yourself a few questions.

Do you want to write a book?

I did. And so I wrote this one in a couple months, and self-published it on Amazon. No publishers necessary.

Do you want to become a musician?

Post 100 videos or song covers to YouTube. Upload the audio to SoundCloud or a similar service. There are bands who make a living online without the expense or logistics of touring.

Do you want to create a community around homebrewing?

Organize an in-person get together through MeetUp.com. Offer advice to newbies and an incentive for people to share with friends. Once you build a tribe, create events and find local breweries to sponsor them.

Technology today allows us to do almost anything we want to do. It's up to you to A) understand where your target audience is, B) find the right combination of tools and content to get in front of them, and C) suck it up and do the initial hard work because there are no shortcuts!

The silver lining is that you pick a subject you enjoy and are passionate about. Then hard work doesn't seem so bad.

Chapter 4 - Identify Your Best Skills

What are you good at?

This isn't the time to be negative, we all have strengths and weaknesses. And if you are creative, you can find ways to work around your weak points.

If you are interested in web design, I'd bet you have one of the following personality types: coder, designer, techie, entrepreneur, extrovert, or salesperson.

I'm a coder/techie, mostly introverted, and thankfully with a semester's worth of experience in Adobe Photoshop and Illustrator.

I didn't know anything about the principles of great design. I didn't know a thing about business.

What I did have was a lot of years using Google and websites as my prime source of learning.

I feel like I've seen 1,000,000 websites over the years, and I have a good idea of how professional level websites look and function.

This is Not a Career Move

You shouldn't view your current interest in web design as a new career.

You might think I'm crazy for saying that, but here's why...

15 years ago it was actually very difficult and expensive to build a large website. You had to know code and your design options were limited. The internet was slower, so high quality images and videos weren't common. E-commerce websites cost thousands of dollars and weeks to setup.

Today, you can buy your domain and web hosting in 10 minutes and setup your website with 1-click. You can publish your first blog post or page within 30 minutes. You can setup an e-commerce store in 30 minutes. Then you can add your products to Amazon/Etsy and sell on multiple platforms in a couple days.

Who knows where we are going to be 10 years from now. Technology improves rapidly and exponentially.

I've already seen numerous ads for a startup which claims your website design will be completely automated with artificial intelligence. Just provide your content and they will do the rest.

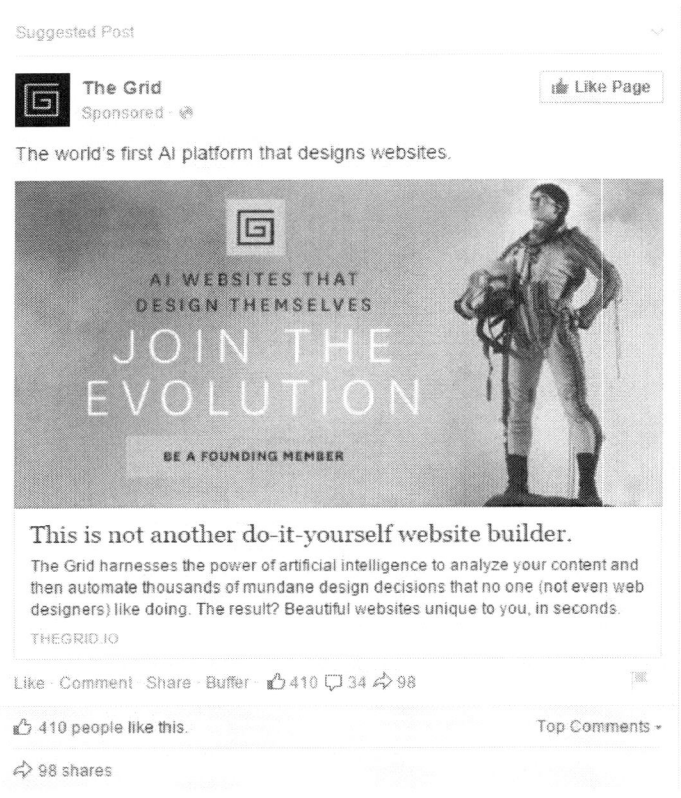

I don't doubt it'll work eventually. They are collecting leads and have a loose launch date of Spring/Summer 2015.

However, I doubt it's going to catch on quickly considering the massive existing footprint of the internet.

I also doubt it's going to run smoothly in those first couple months because what they are trying to do is a massive undertaking.

25

What I do know is business will exist 10 years from now. And on the whole, people are slow to adapt to new technologies. Most begrudgingly do it, only to find it was the best decision they ever made.

Use websites as a vehicle to learning business and higher leverage skills. That is where you will find the bigger pot of gold that the commodity services cannot provide.

What Can You Learn Through a Website?

Code, design, content management, project management, marketing, blogging, copywriting, conversions, selling, paid advertising, social media, generating leads, e-commerce, outsourcing, automating, delegating.

The list goes on.

You want to learn the timeless values that don't change as fast as technology. Techniques and tricks come and go, principles persist through those changes.

It takes a big picture understanding to achieve your highest level of success. This includes marketing, sales, business and really human psychology.

I'm still not there. I'm not sure anyone reaches that point.

Aim to build trust and increase your skill level each day so you become more valuable to the clients who work with you on a regular basis.

You want to build relationships which pay off in more ways than a one-time invoice. This could mean consistent monthly work, referrals, sharing ideas or future projects that you can spearhead.

The key is treating your experiences as a journey of curiosity and improvement. You never know where it's going to lead, but if you have the passion, chances are you'll continue to advance and ultimately get somewhere interesting.

It's up to you to create your own path and find your own way.

Connect the Dots

There are thousands of unbelievable resources at your fingertips today that simply didn't exist 5 years ago.

Several are listed in the resources section at the end of this book.

The way to set yourself apart is to find the handful of tools you can master to help other people.

For instance, if it's a fashion business, you need to learn Pinterest and Instagram marketing because great photos spread like wildfire there. But you can avoid a largely text based communication social network such as Twitter when you start out. That way you can focus your time on the higher leverage work.

On the flipside, if your content is 90% informative articles or blog posts, Twitter is the ideal place to build your audience.

By gaining a deeper understanding of a couple platforms that align with your specific niche, you'll have the advantage over competitors that offer any service to any type of business.

The one absolute necessity for every business is a website.

The social platforms can supplement your marketing plans and drive traffic. But if you rely on a 3rd party platform, they can change their rules or algorithm and cut you off from future business.

Ask Facebook page owners who were recently informed they need to pay to reach most of the people who "liked" their page.

They were laughing all the way to the bank, proclaiming Facebook is the easiest way to make money. Then they were hit with a dose of reality and needed to shift to stay afloat.

Some will learn, others will complain and blame Facebook. The latter are the ones that do not succeed long-term.

That's business. If you don't own it, you don't control it. And you are a slave to their rules. A website and an e-mail list are really the only two things you "own" online and can move from one platform to another.

Use that fact to your advantage when approaching a potential client and pitching web services.

Chapter 5 - Pick a Platform and Master It

In my humble opinion, there are only a handful of reasons to not use WordPress as the framework for your website.

Why Use WordPress.org

Let me first go over some of the most recent stats from 2015.

Of the top 10,000,000 websites by traffic, 20% use WordPress.

Of the top 1,000,000 websites by traffic, 50% use WordPress including NY Post, Time.com, CNN, USA Today, NBC Sports, and Spotify.

If we are just looking at content management systems and not all types of websites, WordPress is closer to 50% which dwarfs the runner-up (Drupal) at under 15%.

Bottom line, unless you are doing some type of uber-custom website, stick with WordPress and its massive community for the best long-term experience.

There is a learning curve to master it, but it's really easy to get started.

Why is WordPress So Popular?

The reason is simple - it's completely open-source.

If you are unfamiliar with that term, it means that all of the source code used to build WordPress is available to the public.

Thousands upon thousands of people smarter than me are able to: spot flaws then report them to increase security, develop and design themes to give your website an amazing look, and create plugins that add a new level of functionality to your website.

If you can think of it, a plugin probably exists to add it to your website.

However, there is a good chance you are more familiar with services like Wix, Squarespace or Weebly.

That's because WordPress doesn't spend nearly any money for advertising.

While the others are shelling out $4.5 million to get a 30-second spot on the NFL Super Bowl, WordPress lets the software itself do the selling.

And it works.

It's morphed from a blogging platform only to one of the best frameworks you can select for your personal, business or client website.

Have a question about how something works? There's a good chance it's been answered on a forum already.

The level of documentation of WordPress compared to the other website services is not comparable. That is because there is a community of WordPress enthusiasts happy to help, myself included.

I wouldn't be writing this book if it wasn't for WordPress.

What I've learned is that you can do almost anything with WordPress, but it can be difficult to find the exact instructions you need within the sea of information. Sometimes you need to dig into code to really perfect a project.

Give it time, the more you learn, the easier it is to come up with a solution to your specific problem.

One caveat that you need to know - DO NOT use WordPress.com

This is a great choice for a free personal blog, however it's on their web hosting servers, and you have a very limited set of options to customize your website.

It's not an ideal way to learn WordPress for client websites.

Instead, get your own web hosting and install WordPress software found on WordPress.org.

If you use HostGator like I do, you can install WordPress in about 1-minute with QuickInstall, through your cPanel account.

Utilize Your Strengths

The other beautiful aspect of WordPress is that you can let your best skills shine. The software and framework take care of a lot of the mundane details of managing a website. Plus you have options when putting together a website.

Are you great at design?

Then create a custom look in Photoshop and outsource the conversion from PSD to a WordPress theme. Or learn CSS so you can become a ninja with tweaking the design exactly how you want it.

Amazing at code?

Buy a pre-made WordPress theme and hack the PHP theme files to add really unique features. Then find businesses that need these features added to their existing WordPress website. Or you can delve into the world of WP plugin development.

Are you an entrepreneur or hustler?

Find a great premium WordPress theme, do a little customizing for one type of industry like landscaping, then call a list of 100-200 and sell them the website with a monthly maintenance and hosting fee.

Are you an introvert (like me)?

Utilize your personal network as much as possible, because it helps to have others champion for you. Once you do great work for a couple people, they will gladly refer you to other people they know. You can build up a side income and start a business the old fashioned way - through local referrals. You will become more comfortable talking and selling when you have mastered some aspect of your platform.

It's not what everyone dreams. You are probably envisioning it right now, living like a king and operating your business from the pristine beaches of Hawaii. Margarita in your hand, ass in the sand.

It is possible, but that takes a lot of hard work and perseverance to reach that point. Passive money is the ultimate goal, but it's a lot easier to get paid today for a unique service that you bring to the table.

What we want to focus on are the plenty of business owners in your town or niche who would clearly benefit from you taking over their online marketing.

If you have used Facebook or Google extensively, you have superior skills than these offline business folks!

Start off with small goals and make a little improvement each day.

Otherwise Hawaii will always be a dream and no closer to reality.

When NOT to Use WordPress.org

Despite my love of WordPress, I understand there are times when it's not appropriate.

It's all about the best solution for your idea or business concept.

Here are instances when you need to shy away from a content management system like WordPress:

- **Custom Web App or SaaS** - Think of Twitter or Hulu as examples. Other SaaS (Software as a Service) business models will require custom programming using PHP or Ruby on Rails.
- **Major E-Commerce Website** - You remember those WordPress plugins I mentioned? There are plenty of great options for e-commerce. However if you are selling a high volume of items or have a huge inventory, you are better off using a framework specifically designed for e-commerce like Shopify.
- **Simple Websites** - WordPress can be overkill for a 1-2 page brochure website or landing page that you know won't be updated much, if at all. An HTML/CSS template is probably the better option in this scenario.
- **Photo & Video Heavy Websites** - Again, this can be accomplished with WordPress using themes and plugins, however it's not the best match in terms of managing multimedia without much text.
- **Fully Custom Design** - If you have a unique design, you must consider whether it's worth it to convert to a WordPress theme vs. HTML/CSS on a case-by-case basis.

Your best option is digging in with WordPress since it's free, and learning through experience.

When you do that, you'll begin to understand it's limitations, which are getting fewer by the day.

For what I build with small business websites, there couldn't be a better match than WordPress.

Chapter 6 - Fundamentals of Business

Whether you are starting a web design business on the side to supplement your job income, or diving in full-time from the beginning, you need to learn new skills.

You know how to create websites, but you are entering a new realm involving accounting, marketing, advertising, sales, customer support, project management and leadership.

It's not an easy transition, and you will make mistakes along the way.

I spent $1,500 on a payroll service company because I didn't understand tax withholding. Turns out it was a complete waste of money. As a one-man business owner, I can write a check from the business account to my name and classify it as an "owner distribution".

Shout out to my accountant for that tip.

This shows I knew absolutely nothing about accounting, taxes or the simple requirements of running a business.

I'm no expert, but having learned the hard way, I want to share tips so you can navigate a less expensive path.

Increase Cash Flow

Cash, and therefore sales, are the lifeblood of any business. If you don't believe me, I'm giving you homework!

Go watch the TV show "Shark Tank".

Once you see a handful of episodes, you'll notice trends with the questions each "shark" asks after a pitch.

The most common rebuttal you'll hear is, "Yes, but what are your sales this year?"

If you don't have sales, it doesn't matter if you have a well-thought out plan. You don't have a business until you've proved your concept within the market, by getting people to trade their hard-earned cash for your product or service.

The nice thing about web design is that it can be a high-end service. You don't need 100's of sales to bring in serious cash. And you don't need to invest your life savings to get started.

The ultimate goal is to become a website marketing expert so you implement your own ideas and get paid $100 - $1,000 per month for each client. They will gladly pay this if you are making them more money.

At the beginning, focus on getting your first couple clients, particularly through your personal network.

They may not be your ideal profile or offer the best pay, but you will gain experience.

If you are going to do work at a lower cost, make sure the project tasks are mutually agreed upon before you start work. Otherwise you may be working on an endless to-do list without a real purpose.

This isn't a recipe for learning or profiting.

Your time is money, so be vigilant of that fact from day one.

You are the Salesperson

I read a book recently which described that in all small businesses, the CEO/owner should be the head of sales until at least $10 million in revenue.

Salesmanship is arguably the most difficult aspect of business to master, because it requires you to actively push someone to make a decision.

Most people would rather let their work speak for itself and sell passively.

I'm no different.

With an engineering background, I'd much rather stay in my home office for 4 straight hours, put music on, and get to work without any interruptions. No human contact.

Unfortunately, it's difficult to achieve that peace at the beginning.

You need to be making connections, sending personal e-mails, making uncomfortable phone calls, answering uncomfortable questions, asking people for the sale, etc.

Don't be overwhelmed. I'm the definition of an introvert and it can drain my energy doing these things.

But I'm also very dedicated to learning about websites and online marketing, plus I'm honest. So I push forward in some way everyday, even if I'm not in sales mode.

If you can show results, it's way easier to break the ice with someone, and they are more likely to respond positively.

Think Like the Customer

The secret in business is in the communication.

Communication builds relationships. Communication sets expectations. Communication relieves people's anxiety.

How you approach your communication with the customer is incredibly important. And it's something I put zero thought into at the beginning. Math, science and numbers were my thing, not words.

It truthfully can be boiled down to this nugget - be authentic, listen to them, and illustrate exactly how your product or service will benefit their lives.

Don't talk about yourself or your business too much. Don't run through the features of your service. That's what I did since it's what I was most excited about.

And definitely do not undercut your desired price to get a quick sale. That's a race to the bottom.

When you are selling a website, you aren't really selling a website at all.

You are selling a business owner on the potential for more customers, more sales and the relief of having an expert (you) manage it for them. Learning about this would take them days, weeks or months, and they cannot afford to spend that time. So they choose to spend their money to get the job done by a trustworthy partner.

It may sound cheesy, but pay attention to infomercials. Ads on TV cost a lot of money, so if they are shown repeatedly, it's obvious people are buying.

Watch how they choose the wording and sell you on how great your life will be with the product.

It can be a non-stick frying pan, copper athletic band, or a home security system. It doesn't matter, but I'd bet each of them show happy people, happy families and a sense of well-being.

Direct response copywriters create those scripts, and the best in this field do well because they strike the core emotion of the customer with their message.

Solve Their Problem

If you want to generalize, you can consider yourself an online problem solver.

Once you have a client, they will ask you questions about new features they want to add to the website. They may have read an article about a new service. Sometimes you won't have experience or know how to implement their ideas.

Don't turn them down immediately. This may be an opportunity to expand your boundaries and expertise.

There is a concept in business called "minimum viable product".

What this means is you have an idea for a business or service. You may even brainstorm 100 ideas that would be worthwhile to implement.

But let's go back to fundamental #1... we need cash, and we need it as fast as possible.

So you have to decide the small subset of features or elements that need to be in place to get the project done as quickly as possible.

Time is always your enemy in business. The longer you take, the more competitors you'll have. And the fastest to market is often the one that wins.

The reason they win is not because their product/service is superior. It's because they get sales the fastest, and get customer feedback first. Then they improve on their initial offering to better solve the customer's problem. The problems that they directly indicated they had, not your hunch.

This iterative process has defined almost every successful company in their early stages. Sometimes the end product is 100% different from the original idea.

Reid Hoffman, the co-founder of LinkedIn, has a wonderful quote to drive this theory home: "If you are not embarrassed by the first version of your product, you've launched too late."

Don't worry about getting it perfect, just get it out there when it works. You can always improve later.

Once you know how to build a website, start to see who needs one. Ask your family, ask your friends.

After you build a handful, start going to businesses and see if they want to work with someone locally.

Once you work with a couple clients, you'll begin to more deeply understand their niche-specific customer problems and be better suited to solve them.

You'll reach the highest level of the totem pole when you learn to drive traffic and get them more business, which is every client's #1 problem.

Reinvest in Yourself

If you start making money, it is natural to get comfortable and stop pushing yourself. With technology, the pace is so rapid that you have to keep looking for the next wave.

This means staying on top of the trends in your niche, and using the newest tools to gain a competitive edge on those who are unwilling to adapt. Don't be afraid to spend money if it's going to greatly benefit your client's and save you time.

10 years into my journey, I've learned so much in a wide array of topics. Now I better understand how those topics fit together to form the online footprint of a business and drive sales.

But it wasn't always that way. I dove deeply into one specific area for weeks at a time until I felt completely comfortable. I would then figure out small ways to test what I was learning, and then used the test results to help direct any future efforts.

As an example, I built a website for a roofer as my first paid project. This was with HTML/CSS.

I then learned PHP and jQuery because you can do more with less lines of code, and I'm all about efficiency. I built a few personal websites using these technologies.

Then I started testing out WordPress for content management. It didn't take me long to become enamored with the ease of use compared to manual coding.

My next couple client websites were built using WordPress, and I even created the PHP theme files from scratch to learn how they worked.

I started to get tired of manual coding because clients didn't care how much effort I put into the back-end. As long as the website looked nice and got them more leads, they were happy. Plus content and search optimization play a much more important role in getting traffic than efficient HTML/CSS/PHP code.

Once I felt like an expert with WordPress, I advanced to higher level online marketing topics. Then I asked my clients if they wanted to start increasing their reach using Google AdWords and Facebook Advertising.

Some didn't want to get involved, but others were 100% on-board. And since they didn't know anything, it was up to me to manage these accounts and understand the platforms.

What I'm getting at here is you want to let your curiosity and also your client's needs fuel your learning path.

Too many people want a roadmap to success, and it simply doesn't exist.

Success in anything comes from passion and the desire to help others. Let your current passion start your journey and be open to learning new things along the way, because every new path is an opportunity.

Freelancer vs. Business Owner

There is a subtle difference between a freelance web designer and an owner operating a web design business.

If you are a freelancer, you have the following characteristics:

- You sell your time
- You do all the work

- You are paid in full after each project

As a business owner, there is a slight shift:

- You sell on value
- You delegate time-consuming tasks
- You generate recurring income

Freelancing has its perks, though.

There is no easier way to make your first dollar. All small business owners wear several hats. Most don't have a complete grasp on marketing or the power of the web. Once you learn a subset of tools, offer your services.

But always have in mind that you want to transition to a business owner mindset with more experience.

It can be difficult to separate the creative work from the business owner role with web design. I love getting into the code or taking the time to make something perfect. But it's important to standardize and re-use as many elements as you can to streamline your process.

If you take the extra step to document your process, it will be that much easier to improve it with each new project. And you can figure out the steps you hate doing, then outsource.

Also, don't overlook the knowledge you can gain from your clients. They already have a taste of success as a business owner. Your job is to increase their success online, while also learning as much as you can about how they grew their business offline.

Many of my clients have had an enormous impact on how I view the duties of a business owner.

Chapter 7 - Getting Your First Client

To be a successful freelancer or create your own business from scratch, you must be committed.

Committed to your craft, committed to your clients, and most importantly committed to yourself.

If you truly believe you have a valuable skill to offer that would benefit another business, don't be afraid to let them know.

Here are 5 specific ways to land your first client as a web designer.

TIP #1: Get Attention

One of my favorite guys to learn from on getting leads and closing sales is Grant Cardone. He's energetic and has that "in your face" personality. It's easy to see why he is great at selling.

However, you don't need to imitate him in your first meeting to make a sale. I'm much more low-key than that dude.

The fact he drives home is you need to grab someone's attention first. The marketplace is more crowded than ever. That's a positive and negative - there are plenty of potential customers but they are being sold to every day, becoming better at spotting the BS.

It's essential that you stand out in some way.

If your service is based on imitating another business, you've lost the battle. The war ain't over yet, though.

Instead, pick a niche that you are interested in and master it. Maybe you are passionate about living an organic lifestyle, so you can seek out those that share the same values as you.

Or you just bought a fixer-upper home and you are learning the ins-and-outs of residential contractor work. I have the most clients in this niche, and I specifically chose them because I knew the lingo after watching an absurd amount of HGTV to learn about home projects. Property Brothers, anyone?

This alone will set you apart from 80% of the pack and make a more memorable first impression.

Here's another big hint – the easiest way to differentiate yourself is to put personality into your work.

Big brands try to do it and it's effective (think Flo from Progressive). This is also why the small guy can compete. You become the face(s) of the business which creates more trust.

Once you've been around the block a couple times, people will know and like you.

TIP #2: Use Your Personal Network

Speaking of knowing and liking, the easiest and often most overlooked way to acquire your first client is through family or friends.

It's not the sexy method, yet it works for one simple reason – people do business with other people they know, like and trust. Regardless of changing technology and new marketing strategies, this underlying truth will remain.

Another great aspect is the lower level of competition. For instance, I'm not familiar with any family members or friends who have the experience I do building websites.

Focus on what you can do today.

Most of us have at least 100-200 friends on Facebook, so that's an ideal place to start.

But don't send out a generic "blast" or status update. Select the people who either work for themselves, are passionate about a subject and might need a website, or have a large network that you could tap into.

Depending on how close you are, contact them as "personally" as you can. Obviously for family and close friends you can either call or send a text message.

For acquaintances and people who you have met through school or other professional endeavors, send a quick email, explaining that you are looking to offer your services. If they don't need help, see if they can refer you to a connection of theirs that does.

It would be shocking if you don't get at least a handful of leads from your own personal network.

In my case, the first person that I did hourly work for was my cousin-in-law. I didn't seek him out. Instead, I would casually talk with him about what I was learning with websites at family parties, and then ask him questions about his business.

At the time I didn't think of it. But these were essentially sales conversations.

He is a one-man operation and outsourced his website to Italy in the years prior. He eventually decided he wanted help with someone local and started sending work my way.

Even if it's family, money is money!

Plus it's easier to get testimonials from people that you have an existing relationship with. This way you can add social proof to your portfolio website quickly and show that you can deliver.

TIP #3: Go the Extra Mile (And Be Memorable)

As mentioned in tip number one, your advantage is the personal touch. So whenever possible, take the extra step to set yourself apart.

Some examples of this may include:

- **Build a Demo Website First** – Most people have the general pitch of, "I can build you a website". If you flip it by saying, "I put together a mockup of what your site will look like with your logo, take a

look", folks are much more likely to respond positively.
- **Show Your Face** – Besides your personal network, the next easiest method to finding a client is talking in person with a decision-maker. Take a stroll down main street and drop in a few places to introduce yourself. They will remember you, especially if you are their customer. It's not a hard-sell but a "get to know you" conversation.
- **Be Human** - Once your email address is out there on your website, you become immune to seeing bad cold emails for SEO, web development services, graphics and everything else. Why not send a handwritten letter to 20 businesses that you specifically target? That should be more effective than emailing 1,000 with a generic template.
- **Do Your Homework** - The more you can make it about them, the better. Check out their current website, see how long they've been in business, find out if they are active on social media, etc. Then compliment them or offer practical advice based on your research before jumping into any sales pitch.
- **Follow Up** – We're all busy. And we all forget things. If they show interest in working with you but you don't hear from them, it never hurts to touch base after a couple days. Send a quick 1-2 line email or give them a call to understand what is holding them back from making a decision.

TIP #4: Sell Results, Not Features

When you first learn various website design techniques, you have a tendency to want to talk about what you can do.

But it's always best to avoid technical jargon. Instead focus on the outcomes the client will see from your work.

For example, discuss how a website is going to improve their brand online and drive more local traffic which will lead to new clients.

Don't go on and on about how fast you can make the site load or the cool slider image gallery you built.

You and I both know it's awesome and it needs to load fast, however we are selling results, not features.

And the truth is, most clients don't care about what's going on behind the scenes. (the code, the icons choices, and so forth.) They want to achieve their number one business goal — which is always more leads and sales.

This is why it's important to specialize as you gain more experience. When you begin to understand one industry and their specific goals, you will start to talk their language and become an "insider".

Then when you get tangible results for your first couple clients, you and your skillset will become much more relevant and powerful when you approach the next client.

The key takeaway here is that when "selling", emphasize the results your clients are hoping to achieve (like more customers). Not features of the website.

Chapter 8 - Pricing Structures and Payments

How much does a website cost?

That's the question client's ask the most to start off a conversation.

It's also what people learning web design want to know because they are interested in how much money they can make by selling websites to local businesses.

The answer that no one wants to hear - it depends!

You could find a number of people who will create a simple website for free with future upsells, to $10,000 depending on the project scope and complexity.

My dad is vice president of a large safety products company with warehouses all over the country. Their website has an online store for service professionals. He told me their website revamping was going to cost over $100,000 and almost a year to complete.

That's a bigger job than any freelancer could handle, but it shows you the disparity of price depending on the business type.

Having said that, I recommend two things:

<u>DO NOT Charge Per Hour</u>

Think about your hourly rate, but do everything you can to charge by project instead of per hour.

The reason for that is simple.

When a client hears our project price they know what they are going to pay in advance. It gives them a reference point that they can wrap their head around.

On the other hand with an hourly rate, you may do the work upfront and then send an invoice, but if it wasn't clear how long it would take, they may have "sticker shock".

And obviously over time, you're going to get better at whatever you're doing, so you shouldn't get compensated less when you become more efficient per hour.

DO NOT List Your Prices

People will inevitably go on your website to see what they are in for.

Don't tell them.

It could be a one-page brochure website, you might need to setup an e-mail signup form with an auto-responder sequence, you may need to do advanced tracking, you may be working on an e-commerce website selling physical products.

Bottom line, it's best to have a conversation with your potential client before giving them a price range. That way, you understand what work you have to perform before launching the website.

An exception to this is a fixed monthly service (for $99 or $149/month) where you standardize your offerings. In this case, you may want them to sign-up and pay online instead of calling for a custom consultation.

If you're going down that route, be extremely specific with what comes in each monthly package. And work hard at marketing, because it's difficult to get someone to shell out $1,000+ per year without having a discussion first!

I would also be sure to include some custom or personal features into a monthly package. Otherwise, you will be competing on price with the big companies, and they will destroy you in that market.

Cheap Prices = Cheap Customers

The less you charge, the more your client will attempt to take advantage of you. Psychologically it is odd, but the more you pay for something, the more you value that service.

If you have a cheap price, people are going to see how much they can squeeze out of you.

Whereas if you price yourself at a premium level, it does two things: 1) Provides a larger barrier to entry to fend off potentially bad clients, and 2) Gives you more leeway to over-deliver and provide the "wow" factor to please your best clients.

This can be a hard concept to really let sink in, and even harder to implement.

You may need to tap into your personal network for the first couple jobs to build your portfolio before you feel comfortable asking for a higher rate or price. But one way or another, you need to get to that premium level because if you're the lowest-cost, you are a commodity and replaceable.

The perfect examples of this are big service companies offering the lowest level website creation packages like Squarespace, Yellowpages, Vistaprint, and GoDaddy. They usually start at $10-20/month but you still need to maintain the website yourself.

You are looking for the business owners that want no parts of that.

There's plenty of them in the real world, and they are the people you want to become an asset for, and build an on-going relationship with. You will build trust along the way and they are the ideal clients that will actually value what you do.

Instead of seeing a website as a commodity which they can update themselves, they see the benefit of having you manage their website as a lead generation method in the marketing toolbox.

It's hands off and they can focus on what they do best, not learning something they aren't interested in maintaining.

Client Questionnaire

Part of earning more money per project as a web designer is increasing your efficiency.

This can be difficult with some web design clients. If you make websites for any business under the sun, chances are you are doing a unique set of tasks on every project.

Custom equals time. Time equals money. If you enjoy creating something 100% from scratch for every client, then you need to charge a nice chunk of change for the time and care that go into the creation.

However, if you are looking for more productivity, the easiest way to accomplish this is by using a web design client questionnaire.

By asking your client specific questions about their website vision, you will be in a much better position to understand the scope of work and charge accordingly.

Below are the main questions to ask your web design clients so you can provide an accurate quote.

COMPANY INFORMATION

- List all of the following: Company Name, Address, Phone and Website (if available)
- What year was the company founded?
- Do you have a company logo or preferred colors?
- List all primary contacts: Name, E-mail and Phone
- List all of your services/products that you want included on the website
- List all nearby cities, towns or counties within your service area
- What differentiates you from your competition?
- What types of advertising do you use now, or have you used in the past?

WEBSITE CONTENT

- Do you have a domain and/or website hosting?
- What is the main goal of the website? (i.e. phone calls, e-mail leads, sell products)
- List all pages you want on your website
- Do you want a contact form on your website?
- Do you want to list any organizations you are part of?
- Do you have social media accounts that you want to link?
- If you have website stats, how many visitors do you get each month?
- If you have website stats, what is your main source of traffic?
- Do you have text, photos and/or testimonials ready for the website?
- Do you have videos to feature on your website?
- How often do you plan to update the website content after launch?
- Do you have other marketing materials (i.e. brochures) to use as inspiration for the website design?
- Do you have 2-3 websites that you would like to emulate?
- What is your target date for launching the website?
- If your ideal customer was searching for you, what would they type into Google? Please list 5-10 that come to mind

Download the book bonus package, including this PDF Questionnaire:

http://websiteprofitcourse.com/bb/

When you have an idea what the project entails and you present your proposal with the price, make sure you give them a bulleted list with everything that's going to come with the website. If you don't, people are going to push you to do more, or say, "Oh, I thought this feature was included with the price".

Bottom line, be very clear about what needs to be accomplished so you both fully understand the project.

That includes a list of things they need to provide you.

For example, include that the website will be 10-pages, one layout for the homepage with a featured image, another layout for all the inner pages, 1 company e-mail address (something@theirdomain.com), 1 contact form which forwards to their e-mail, and they must provide all the photos and wording for the website. Simple, yet provides a solid structure for what you need to accomplish and what isn't within the scope of the contract or "handshake" agreement.

Determining the Project Cost

Pricing is ultimately determined by two factors:

#1 - The Value to the Client

#2 - Your Own Value on Your Time

Notice how neither of these relate to the actual details of the website.

Let's start with your time...

I want you to think about how long it's going to take you to complete the project. List out the high-level steps that you need to accomplish, i.e. register domain, setup website hosting, install WordPress, find a professional theme, customize with their logo and colors, build out pages XYZ etc.

Once you come up with the estimated hours it will take, double it. Or at least tack on a few extra hours, because chances are you will underestimate the effort and communication required at the beginning.

I find this to be true with myself, even to this day. Be careful of being overly ambitious and under pricing yourself.

Now that you have an idea of how long it's going to take, how much do you want to make per hour? What is going to pay for your expenses and your lifestyle?

This isn't about being a baller and charging $150/hour from Day 1.

It's about knowing you have a valuable skill to offer, and in order to use that skill for someone else's business, they need to compensate you to live comfortably.

That may be $25/hour now, but it can change at any time or for every new potential client – it's completely up to you. That's also why I recommended keeping your prices guarded.

Multiply your desired rate by the estimated hours, i.e. $100/hour X 10 hours = $1000

Obviously over time as you get better at what you do, you will increase your hourly rate and also find ways to become more efficient throughout the creation process. This may involve creating a systematic process that you follow each project, or it could simply be outsourcing the repetitive tasks.

Now that we discussed your own time value, what is the value to the client?

As a real world example, a website for a newly created yoga studio will not be as valuable as one for an established divorce lawyer. The lawyer may get clients paying them $10,000 – $20,000 each, so getting leads to them through their website is extremely valuable.

You want to focus on the businesses that already have money coming in offline, and would greatly benefit from adding a website to their marketing arsenal. Those are the businesses that have the willingness to pay you and that get the most value out of your services.

And the nice thing is that these small business owners are often much less of a hassle than dealing with a large company.

They don't have elaborate technical ideas that will be over your head, they don't need to have a meeting to make a decision, they don't micromanage what you do.

They will let you do your thing, ask for a quick run down, and even fund your ability to learn and test new online marketing strategies!

Other Pricing Structures

As I mentioned before, you want to price by the project and not by the hour. Most of the time you'll need to have a conversation with the client before you decide on a price range, but another alternative is to "productize" your services.

A great example of this is creating a standard business package website for $2,000 - $3,000 that includes up to 10 pages, paired with domain registration, hosting, Facebook page and cover photo, logo design, business cards, etc.

Make it a unique package that will set them up for success online.

Then if they don't want to manage the website or social media accounts, guess who can do that for a monthly charge?

The great thing about the web is even though there's a million services, you're the one that's going to hand select which ones best fit your clients and manage them with a human touch.

As you get experience, you'll learn which methods are working best and you can double-down on those to see better results.

Accepting Payments

Lastly (but some would say most importantly), how do I get my money?!?

I personally like to charge 50% upfront and the remaining 50% is due on or before launch day.

Other than exchanging information and ideas, I won't work before getting paid. There's too many flaky people to do work without knowing the money is coming.

There are always exceptions to the rule, but it's more important with new clients that you don't fully trust yet.

As a personal warning, I've had multiple business owners that have paid me the initial 50% deposit, I finished 90% of the website, and they wouldn't get in touch with me to put the final touches on the last 10%.

It was always, "Let's review it soon" or "I'll have those pictures over to you next week". It became a long game of back and forth where nothing was accomplished.

At that point, you have to realize that you are wasting time chasing money. But I wasn't empty handed, I still made an OK hourly rate despite never launching those websites since I collected the deposit.

I've accepted payments in a number of ways - cash, check, credit card, money order and even a barter of services in the early days.

A few online payment options you can use are: PayPal, Stripe, Square and Google Wallet.

However, some offline clients will insist on their preferred method, whether it is cash or a written check that you need to go to their office to pick-up.

Don't view this as a hassle. Instead, view it as a way to learn more about their business and build a relationship with them.

When to Avoid a Formal Contract

The other related lesson here is that money is more powerful than a contract.

People often fret when it comes to doing a website without a contract or they spend weeks overthinking what should be in a contract instead of meeting business owners who need a website.

Let me say this with the caveat that a contract of some sort (it can simply be an e-mail) is essential to turn a client down for work that wasn't included with the original price. You can point to it and say, "I told you XYZ would be in there, and doing what you are requesting is more work than we agreed to".

But think about a situation where someone stiffs you, like my situation described above. Are you really going to get a lawyer involved because they didn't follow the contract (which stipulates the project must be completed/paid in 90 days)?

Unless we are talking in the multiple thousands or higher, the answer is no. It's not worth the time, effort or money unless it's a large sum of cash.

FYI, I had a signed contract for both jobs where they ultimately blew me off. I've had zero contracts and zero problems with my best clients.

Meet people face-to-face to build a level of trust as a human. Or if that's not possible, make sure they give you those Benjamins before you get your butt to work!

My first two customers went from one-time project work to a paid monthly retainer where I work on essentially whatever I see fit. That's a much better situation than trying to be a master of litigation, let me tell you.

When you get a few raving clients like that, you'll find people are going to come to you because they will refer you.

Ultimately, the best part of working for yourself is the learning experience you have. You work directly with business owners and you should be asking a lot of questions about their business.

Not only will this give you more insight into how you can improve their website for their customers, but you'll also be able to take their stories and use them for your own business.

Plus people like to talk about themselves, so they'll like you even more when you are genuinely interested in them!

You will transition from a web designer only to a local online marketing expert.

Don't pigeonhole yourself or think you don't have what it takes. I felt the same way at the beginning. You will learn a ton from your first handful of websites.

If you want to see a contract I have used in the past, download the book bonus package from my website below.

http://websiteprofitcourse.com/bb/

DISCLAIMER: I am not a lawyer, and this is not legal advice. I am not responsible for any disputes you have with a client.

Chapter 9 - Web Design Process

This is not a detailed "how to build a website" chapter - or book.

However, I wrote a blog post with step-by-step tutorial videos showing how you can setup WordPress using a free theme. If you have zero experience with WordPress, start there (URL below).

http://websiteprofitcourse.com/how-to-build-a-website-with-wordpress/

Working through numerous personal and client websites, I developed a process that I stick with each time I setup a new site.

As a web design business owner or freelancer, you should have three prime objectives.

- Earn as much money per project as possible
- Improve productivity over time, which allows you to charge and earn more
- Go above and beyond to please your client and build trust with them

If you focus on those, you'll have raving clients who are happy to pay you because you offer unmistakable value. If you provide actual results, they will introduce you to other successful people who are a good match for your services.

The way that I work quickly is by utilizing the power of premium WordPress themes. I start with something that already looks professional, and customize it to achieve a unique look. This takes a fraction of the time compared to coding or designing from scratch.

My WordPress premium theme of choice is iThemes Builder and their set of "child themes". Other great options are the Thesis and Genesis frameworks.

iThemes Builder allows you to create elaborate layouts for a website, and manage the majority of it through WordPress widgets as opposed to code.

That's why I believe anyone can learn with enough passion and grit.

Here is my "secret sauce"...

Domain & Web Hosting

I keep things simple here.

If you are targeting small business owners like me, your clients will not care what domain registrar you use. Same goes for hosting service. Ultimately, you will be charging them to handle the technical details.

I tried saving pennies here and there early on using cheaper hosting companies. That came back to bite me because one of them went out of business with no formal acknowledgement to their customer base.

Stick with a big company on both fronts, so you can rest easy for years to come.

GoDaddy

I use GoDaddy for domain registration and management. I'm sure it's the one you are most familiar with considering they have advertised for years now.

They may not be the absolute cheapest, but we're talking about a couple dollars extra a year per domain, it's not life changing money.

Save your time instead and go with them. I like their domain manager and have been using GoDaddy without issue since day one.

HostGator

As for web hosting, I DO NOT recommend GoDaddy. I think they have upgraded their offerings recently, but some of my clients used them and the problems we encountered were disappointing.

Instead, select HostGator. Specifically the "Reseller" package if you are serious about building websites for multiple local clients.

This gives you a chunk of disk space/bandwidth, and you can setup unlimited websites on there. It's up to you to divide the amount of space needed for each website.

In my experience, you can easily create 20-30 (or more) small business websites on a single reseller account.

It all depends on the website traffic and size of each website. For example, if you are uploading high-resolution images on a daily basis, that will greatly increase the space you need when setting up the hosting.

The HostGator reseller package includes two pieces of software that you need to familiarize yourself with - WHM and cPanel.

WHM stands for "Web Host Manager", and this is where you login to create new websites on your reseller account. If an account is reaching its traffic or size limit, you can easily update the settings within here.

You'll receive your login URL and info for WHM when you sign-up with HostGator.

When you create a new website using WHM, you will also go through the process of creating an account for each one.

This is a cPanel account, and you can manage the individual website hosting settings here. The login page will look like:

http://yourdomain.com/cpanel

Some of the features of cPanel include:

- Add e-mail accounts & forwarders
- Manage all files on your web hosting account
- One-click install of WordPress (among other popular software)
- Create subdomains

Once you setup a handful of websites, the process should become second nature. You repeat the same steps while setting up the domain and hosting.

The custom part starts when selecting the WordPress theme and overall website layout.

Installing WordPress

With cPanel you can install WordPress with one-click in about 1 minute.

It's that easy to get a website up and running. No joke.

A couple notes for you:

- Don't use "admin" as your username for security reasons
- Choose a strong password
- I recommend using LastPass to manage cPanel and WordPress accounts

WordPress comes with a free theme pre-installed which is more suited to blogging than a professional business website.

That's why we want to upgrade to a premium theme to give us a better starting point. More on that in a bit…

Finding Relevant Examples

I can't stress this enough, but every business niche will have a unique design aesthetic, unique list of standard pages, and unique end goals.

It's up to you to do the research and take note of the features you want to include within your website.

I like to search for a business that matches the niche of the website I'm building, located a couple of states away. Or a major city across the country.

The main point is that you want to find 2-3 non-competing yet similar examples. Pick the things you like about each of them and come up with a basic layout to use.

Residential contractors, which are my ideal niche, don't care about fancy design, which is a positive for my skillset. They are focused on looking trustworthy via the website, and they want more calls and e-mails.

It's also easy to find hundreds, if not thousands of examples of similar businesses.

Let's take landscaping as an example. If you are in California, search Google out-of-state for "landscaping portland oregon" and "landscaper in charlotte nc". Only look at the first page of Google because analyzing those will give you clues as to why they rank well.

The high rankings could be due to more relevant content on their website, a social following on Facebook or positive reviews on Google+. Be observant, my friends.

You never want to steal someone's complete design or images. I've had that happen to me, it's not a good feeling.

However, there is nothing wrong with being heavily influenced and customizing their best features to match your website!

Choosing a Premium Theme

Once you understand the structure you want, it's time to select your premium WordPress theme.

I exclusively use iThemes Builder child themes, and then customize to achieve my desired look.

There are several reasons why you want to use a paid premium theme vs. a free theme:

- **Quality** - They look and perform better than free themes
- **Support** - Better help and documentation, may include community forum
- **Updates** - New features added and bugs fixed over time
- **Unique** - Way more websites use free themes instead of paid, so you'll stand out
- **Easy** - The added features make it easier to maintain your website
- **Speed** - The more familiar you become with one theme, the faster you will be

In order to learn WordPress, you'll most likely start with a free theme. There is nothing wrong with this because you need time to play around with the WordPress admin area.

But once you advance to building websites for clients, make sure you are using the best platform possible.

Today, this means your own domain/hosting + WordPress + a premium theme + unique customizations + relevant content.

Building the Layout

This is why I love iThemes Builder.

It allows you to create multiple drag-and-drop layouts which you can assign to specific pages.

For instance, you can have a full-width layout, a right sidebar layout, a squeeze page layout, a photo gallery layout, etc. You can build each layout using WordPress "widgets", so you don't need to know code.

With the layouts built, you manually choose which layout each individual page should use.

It's difficult to describe the awesomeness through words.

You can see the end result at my website. I recommend that you download the book bonus package for free goodies (link below), then browse my website.

It's made with iThemes Builder using several unique layouts for the homepage, the blog, and e-mail signup pages:

http://websiteprofitcourse.com/bb/

Adding Pages

Once you have a couple layouts ready, it's time to add the content.

Pull out your filled client questionnaire to get all the information you need to start building the pages.

Standard pages might include: Home, About, Services, Testimonials, Store, Portfolio, Pricing, Contact, FAQ, Resources, Blog, etc.

A common issue with small business clients is they don't have content ready to use for the website.

You may need to improvise and write-up a quick couple of paragraphs or bulleted list to get the website ready. It may not be ideal, but it'll get you closer to receiving your money.

In this scenario, Google is your friend. That's really every scenario, but especially here.

Use these creative search phrases to find examples of copywriting for specific types of pages:

- [city] [state] [business type] inurl:about.html
- [city] [state] [business type] inurl:about.php
- [city] [state] [business type] inurl:about
- [city] [state] [business type] inurl:testimonials.html
- [city] [state] [business type] inurl:testimonials.php
- [city] [state] [business type] inurl:testimonials
- [city] [state] [business type] inurl:services.html
- [city] [state] [business type] inurl:services.php
- [city] [state] [business type] inurl:services
- [business type] inurl:[page-name]

Adding Plugins

BackupBuddy

BackupBuddy is another wonderful product from iThemes, an automated backup solution that can export to Dropbox.

I set this up on every client website so I have backups available should anything bad happen.

FYI, I haven't had any drastic occurrences yet.

Contact Form 7

This is one of the oldest contact form plugins available on WordPress. It's been around for over 5 years, and I've used it exclusively in that time period.

You can be as simple or elaborate as you want with the forms you build. And you can even track form submissions using Google Analytics to gather more useful data.

Limit Login Attempts

There are hackers out there. It's the way it is on the web.

We need to provide layers of protection across our client websites to counteract these malicious folks.

First, use a strong and unique password.

Next, install this plugin which will lock someone out of the WordPress login page if they type in the wrong password more than a couple times. This is often an automated spambot.

Responsive Lightbox

Do you know the feature where you click on a thumbnail and it expands within the same browser window, with the background greyed out?

It's called the "lightbox" effect.

This is the go-to plugin to accomplish that look on your client's photo gallery or other thumbnails.

Search and Replace

I love this plugin when you need to replace a piece of text or phrase that exists across multiple posts and pages.

Say for instance you want to change the company name from, "Bob's Auto Parts" to "Bob's Auto Parts LLC". There might be 10 instances of this company name on random pages.

This will browse the WordPress database, and replace it for you, just like the search and replace function within a text document.

Simple 301 Redirects

If you are redesigning a website, it is crucial to redirect the existing pages to the new ones.

This is for two reasons:

- **Search Traffic** - If the website has been around for years, chances are it has some traffic through Google. If you completely change the URL structure with your redesign, it can drastically affect your search rankings in Google. You can't afford to mess around here.
- **Existing Links** - There are likely links out there which point back to the old pages. If someone clicks on those links, you don't want them to get a "page not found" message.

In order to streamline this process, I like to make a spreadsheet of all the page URL's currently indexed in Google. Use the following Google search to find these:

site:yourclientdomain.com

Then, if the URL is going to change when you update the website to WordPress, note that URL change in an adjacent column.

You can use the Simple 301 Redirects tool to handle these once you've identified all the pages.

SumoMe

A relatively new plugin, it's one of the coolest I've used in a long time.

They have a suite of tools to better understand your website visitors and convert them to e-mail subscribers.

The following features are included for free:

- **E-mail Popup Box** - It can be mildly annoying, but case studies show they work.
- **Scroll Box** - A visitor who has read your entire blog post is a warm lead, so this tool slides in an opportunity for them to subscribe to your list when they reach the bottom.
- **Heat Maps** - See exactly where people are clicking on your website pages. Amazing.
- **Social Sharing** - Install mobile responsive social sharing buttons to every page on your website.
- **Image Sharing** - Make it easy for your users to share images on Pinterest, Facebook and Twitter.

There are more tools available that I haven't personally used yet, along with paid upgrades to the ones listed above.

TablePress

This plugin makes it easy to insert a table within a WordPress post or page.

A perfect match for pricing, statistics or a comparison chart.

User Role Editor

You can create new administrator or editor accounts if you want to outsource and collaborate on a single WordPress website.

However, there are times when you want to restrict the user's ability to edit some part of the website.

If that is the case, this plugin might be the ideal solution.

I've used this in the past when creating a client's account. If they aren't computer savvy, I don't want them messing around with a setting that can break their website!

WordPress SEO by Yoast

This is a WordPress plugin that is widely known as the only one you need to install for SEO.

It's really cool and not difficult to get started if you know nothing about Google or local search.

After activating the plugin on your WordPress website, you will see a new section added to the bottom of your WordPress pages (see image below).

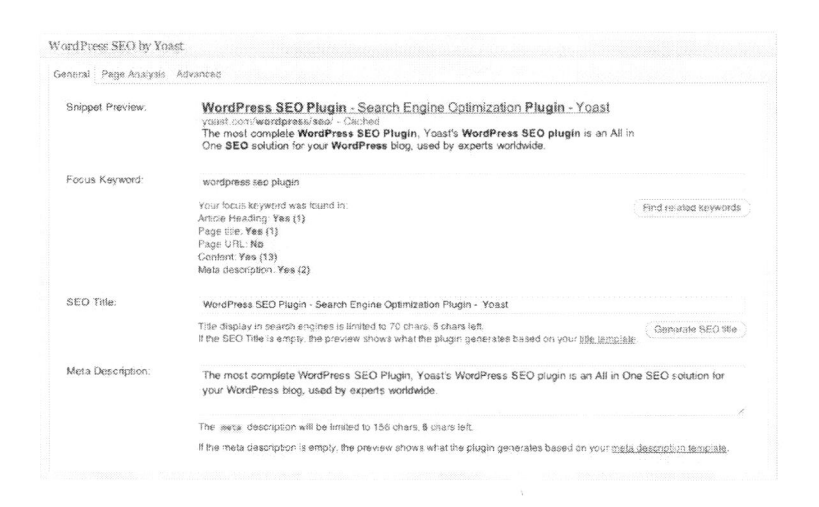

As you can see, it gives you a preview of how your website listing for that page will look in Google.

You can set a "focus keyword" for each page, and the tool will immediately check the various elements on the page to see if your focus keyword appears.

If it's everywhere, you'll see the green "Yes" across the board. If you see the red "No", it helps for SEO to naturally add your focus keyword there, whether it's the page title or URL.

The meta description is almost the same length as a Twitter post, and it's your 1-2 line description of the page that should entice the reader to click. If you don't create a custom meta description, Google will usually select the first line of text from the page.

However, Google may display a unique description for your listing, depending on the actual keyword phrase used to search.

WP Super Cache

This plugin tells the browser to "save" certain images or files locally, so if a user revisits your website, they don't need to load those files from the web server again.

It can be a bit technical, but essentially it's used to speed up your website when you get returning visitors.

Getting Ready to Launch

This is the point where you want to double check the important aspects of the website.

Your task list may include:

- Check all pages
- Verify all links (text, buttons, images)
- Verify 301 redirects work properly
- SEO-friendly pages & posts
- Test responsive design
- Test load time
- Test custom e-mail addresses or forwarding
- Test contact forms

It's natural to spend much time worrying about getting every last detail right - especially on those first couple projects.

It's important, but you can always fix things on the fly.

Do a thorough once-over and get that website live!

Monitoring Post-Launch

This is where you will make your money.

It's worth repeating. The money is in the management.

This is where you separate yourself from the pack of commodity website builders like Squarespace and Wix. They only provide a platform for easy building.

They don't provide a marketing plan specific to one business niche. They don't come up with unique ideas and test them out. They don't give you an outline for driving traffic to the website. They don't provide a custom representative who intimately knows your website.

Some people don't need that level of service. They just want a resume website or something which will never be updated or used to the fullest extent.

That's fine, let them do it themselves at a low cost.

It's your duty to treat every client website like your own, and figure out how to make your clients more successful online. That's when they will become customers for life.

Install Google Analytics

Google Analytics should be installed on every website. It's free, and it gives you unbelievable insight into how your website is working.

There is a saying that goes, "what gets measured gets managed." Google Analytics does the measuring, you need to do the managing.

I'm not going to lie, it can be intimidating to the first time user. The level of detail they provide is overwhelming.

If you are a newbie, I'd recommend focusing on these areas to start:

- **Acquisition > All Traffic > Source/Medium** - This will tell you exactly where your traffic is coming from, whether it's Google search, referrals from another website, social media, or elsewhere
- **Audience > Geo > Location** - See where your visitors are at in the world, down to the city level
- **Audience > Mobile > Overview** - Find out how many people are accessing your website through a desktop, tablet or mobile device
- **Behavior > Site Content > All Pages** - This gives you an overview of how each page on your website is performing

And here is a brief explanation of the important metrics:

- **Pages/Session** - This is how many pages a visitor viewed while on your website

- **Average Session Duration** - How long a user spent on your website, though if they don't go to a 2nd page, this is tracked as 0.
- **Bounce Rate** - This is the percentage of people who visit one page only and then leave, which may actually be the goal on a landing or squeeze page
- **% Exit** - This is the amount of people who exit from a certain page, which can help you understand how to direct visitors from page-to-page

Install on your website and start accumulating data today. The more data you collect, the easier it is to spot trends. That's when the puzzle begins to take shape.

Track Conversions

Google provides a handful of methods to track conversions. What is a conversion?

It could be an e-mail form submit, a list sign-up, an e-commerce sale or a phone call.

The easiest way to do this is create a separate page which users only reach once they complete your goal.

In the example of an e-commerce sale, this would be a "Thank You for Purchasing" page.

You can also track each time someone submits a contact form on your website using Google Analytics paired with the Contact Form 7 WordPress plugin.

I use this exact setup to track contact form inquiries for a handful of my residential contractor clients.

Phone call tracking is a bit more advanced, and I have only tested this using the Google AdWords platform. I anticipate phone call tracking to become easier and more ubiquitous in the next few years.

It goes without saying, but it's much easier to make decisions based on actual results and not what you think will happen. The more you can track (and later analyze) the better off you'll be.

Test Advertising

Once you begin to see visitors on your website, you may want to pump that up with paid traffic.

The two biggest platforms are Google AdWords and Facebook Advertising.

AdWords is heavily based on search intent. You know what the consumer is looking for by what they type into Google.

Facebook is heavily based on demographic targeting. You can pinpoint the exact age range, interests and location of your ideal customer.

But don't limit yourself to those. They tend to be more expensive since they are saturated. All of the social media players have advertising or are developing a platform - Twitter, Instagram, Pinterest, etc.

Then you have mobile advertising platforms to reach people using apps on their phone. In my experience, these are currently filled with mobile app companies and insurance, since they have big marketing budgets to test these new outlets.

There is also display advertising, i.e. banners, which you can setup through Google's Display Network or through independent blogs/websites. One example of a display advertising network is BuySellAds.com.

Make sure to monitor the performance of all campaigns with Google Analytics.

You don't want to try everything at once and not get enough insight into one platform. Start with one at a time until you are comfortable.

With paid advertising, you tend to pay more upfront when you first setup an account. Then as your account accumulates more data and you test more offers, your cost goes down.

There is a fine line between testing to gather data and blowing your budget on a bad ad.

Discuss how much you're willing to test with your client and collectively come up with an attention grabbing ad to kick things off.

Also, tell your client to ask their customers how they found them.

If "Google" or "the internet" becomes a more frequent answer, you'll know you are doing your job.

Monitor Website Traffic

Every couple of months, or each quarter of the year, you should review your client's progress.

See where they are getting their traffic. Come up with ideas on how to improve. It could be adding more content. It might be filming a quick video to add a personal touch to the website. It could be shifting the advertising approach.

Just keep learning and keep trying things. Clients love this. They will treat you like an integral part of their business, not a commodity service.

It's almost like being an employee with benefits. They feel like they have a team member, yet you control of when, where and how you work.

I started off this section by emphasizing this, and I'll end the same way - learn how to drive traffic, monitor, and manage to build success long-term.

I've used a lot of what I learned through client projects, then applied that knowledge to my own personal projects. And vice versa.

The more you learn, the more you do. The more you do, the more that work compounds into wisdom and greater opportunity.

Repurpose From Project to Project

The more times you repeat something, the easier it becomes. This is the case with everything in life.

But you can accelerate that even further by using tiny snippets of existing code, or the same graphics as the base of each website you build.

Every new project, aim to re-use at least one aspect from the previous website.

That way, you are always building on your work instead of creating something new then throwing it away.

I've reused the following:

- HTML Code
- CSS Code
- PHP Code
- jQuery Code
- WordPress Child Themes
- Document Templates
- Spreadsheet Templates
- E-mail Templates

This is the engineer mentality. Once you start to repeat a task, you ask yourself, "how can I automate this or eliminate a step?"

Build a library of templates in all forms - code, text, graphics, communication, etc.

Then when you add new features, think about how you can pull them out from a new project and re-use it (or upsell) across existing client websites.

Chapter 10 - Client & Project Management

I believe the ease or difficulty of managing a client comes down to two elements: the shared expectations and your ability to organize important details.

The more detail oriented you are, the better you will become at handling client issues.

Organize Your Life

If there is one skill I have that stands out above all others, it's my organization.

I despise a mess, whether it's papers spread across a table or 50 random files on my computer desktop. It literally scrambles my thoughts.

When my space is optimized, I think clearly, produce at a higher level, and retain a larger amount of information.

I am a heavy content consumer. I'm always reading new techniques, finding new sources for learning, pushing myself to test new skills. For instance right now it's writing and teaching through video tutorials.

I highly recommend you create a system for every important task you do, and follow it religiously. If you can simplify or automate repetitive tasks, that is even better. It's the #1 thing you can do to increase your productivity.

Let me discuss some of how I like to organize my world. It has a direct relation to organizing my business.

OFFICE & DESK AREA

Multiple Computers - While you can get by with one computer, I think it's nice to have a powerful PC and a portable laptop.

I converted years ago to a Macbook for my laptop, but I still go for the cheap speed/storage of a Windows PC. Without question, I am most productive at my home office while doing my work on a PC.

I use the Macbook for music, casual browsing, and of course working while on the road.

Dual Monitors - It took me a couple years to buy into the dual monitor approach, but when you work on a website, you have multiple programs and browser tabs open.

There are times when I go between the WordPress admin pages, FileZilla, Photoshop, and Chrome Inspector within 5 minutes. Navigating through each of them on a screen with limited real estate becomes a task within itself.

With two monitors, or even three, you can spread things out and keep the big picture fresh in your mind.

Standing Desk - Back when I was learning from my bedroom in my parents house, I came to the conclusion that I sat too much. I would often be at the computer for 2-3 hours at a time, and for multiple periods throughout the day.

When I moved into my own house, my first priority for a home office was a standing desk.

The first couple days are difficult on your feet and legs, especially if you are used to sitting at a computer desk. But once your body adapts, it really does give you more energy and clarity as you perform your daily routine.

If I ever feel sluggish sitting in my chair, I put on music and simply stand to do my work. And about 90% of the time, it reinvigorates me for another hour or two.

Plus it's easier to communicate on the phone while standing. Don't ask me why, but I'm sure you've wandered around the house during a deep conversation!

Mounted Electronics - As you can see above, I have my monitors mounted to the wall so I have the most space on my desk.

I also have bad allergies at times. As a kid, it was worst with pollen during the spring. The last couple years it's been dust on or under my desk, which initiates a sneezing fit. This is especially true during winter when the house gets limited fresh air for three months.

To make cleanup easier, I setup a pegboard with all electronics mounted under my desk. I then slapped together a small shelf for my computer tower.

The result? Nothing touches the rug underneath my desk and it stays much less dusty.

The cables could be better but it's good enough for me.

Idea Folder - This stems directly from listening to James Altucher and buying into his concepts. He wants everyone to focus on their "idea muscle", which will atrophy if you don't exercise it.

The way to make your brain "sweat" is come up with a daily theme, and write 10 ideas.

Some examples include:

- 10 Titles for a Book I Could Write
- 10 Chapters of a Book I Could Write
- 10 TV Shows I Want to See
- 10 Ways Whole Foods Could Get Me to Spend More Money
- 10 Biographies I've Read and What I Learned
- 10 New Features I Can Add to Client Websites
- 10 Ideas to Improve Marketing and Profits at My Company

The point is not to unleash world-class ideas left and right. It's to think clearly about one topic, and exercise your brain until you are out of ideas. At that point, come up with 2-3 more.

Some are good, most are bad.

That's how you improve. If you go for sheer quantity, you are bound to come up with a few winning ideas that ignite passion within you.

You will know when to act and take the next step. The execution steps are just another set of ideas.

This book is a direct result of ideas I've written down on paper, starting with the table of contents. It took me down a path where I felt obligated to tell my story and give back to others who want to learn what I know.

The power is in documenting your thoughts. We all have good ideas bouncing around our brain, we simply forget them. When inspiration strikes, write it down immediately.

File Cabinet - I have an offline aspect to my business, namely promotional products. A necessary evil of this business is a lot of physical mail and paperwork.

Even if 95% of your business is online, chances are there are some documents that you need to organize around your desk like bills, statements, etc.

Don't throw them into a pile and forget about them. Use a simple folder or filing system. It can be as easy as manila file folders like my idea folder pictured above. That's what I use in conjunction with a filing cabinet.

COMPUTER FILES & FOLDERS

Desktop - The desktop on my computer is a lot like the desk in my office. It's my scratchpad while I'm working on a project. Then, once it becomes a bit of a mess, I file the important documents into a more organized folder structure.

When you have a folder structure in place, keeping things organized becomes easy.

I can pinpoint a random client PDF file from 4 years ago in seconds. Boom!

Folder Structure - My important files are in my Dropbox folder so they backup to all my computers (more on that in the next section). I have a top-level folder within Dropbox for all my web design business files.

When I first set this up, I created subfolders for files relating to the following categories:

- **Adobe Illustrator** - Free and custom vector files.
- **Adobe Photoshop** - Same concept as above with PSD files.
- **Background Patterns** - Subtle and repeating backgrounds to use for websites.
- **Books** - e-Books and PDF files.
- **Clients** - Create subfolders for each client, use for photos, files, and documents.
- **Company Files** - Your business logos and important documents.
- **Fonts & Typography** - Free font downloads or typography cheat sheets.

- **Marketing** - Various marketing ideas, described in the next section.
- **PHP** - Tutorials and code samples.
- **SEO Resources** - Cheat sheets, notes, etc.
- **Snippets** - Code to reuse by copying/pasting.
- **Tutorials** - Videos or written tutorials.
- **WordPress** - Themes, plugins and cheat sheets.

Use this as a template for your folder structure and improve based on how your brain operates!

Business - Let's dig into my "Company Files" and "Marketing" folders. Those are really the meat when it comes to the business side.

Here are the subfolders:

- **Backups** - Website backup files, automatically scheduled using BackupBuddy WordPress plugin
- **Business Cards** - Ideas and templates.
- **Cold Calling** - Example MP3 recordings and cold-call scripts.
- **Consultation** - Handouts for meetings and big picture concepts to convey.
- **Contract** - Examples of web design contracts and your custom version.
- **Inspiration** - Ads that catch your eye, i.e. Flyers, Postcards, Facebook, Banner, etc.
- **Logos** - Different versions of your business logo for website, social accounts, etc.
- **Resources** - Website creation process list, plus other tools/spreadsheets.

- **Sales** - Sales letters, lead lists, goals, projections and price charts.
- **WordPress Website Files** - All files used to design your website. I also create this as a subfolder within each client folder.

Personal - My desire to be organized stems from my personal life, not my business life. I have a folder on my Dropbox called "Shared", and I put non-business files in there.

As always, this isn't a dumping space, there is a method to the madness. Here are the subfolders:

- **Backgrounds** - I keep all wallpapers for my PC and Macbook in this folder.
- **Banks & Finance** - Account statements, expense list, utility payments, etc.
- **DIY Household Products** - I'm into organic alternatives to common items, i.e. cleaning sprays. I gather and create concoctions here.
- **DIY Projects** - These are any house projects that require a little planning, i.e. gardening, landscaping, etc.
- **Fantasy Football** - I love playing with my longtime friends. And I wrote a short e-book on the topic to test Amazon self-publishing. I don't mean to brag, but over the past 5 years I have dominated my league!
- **Food** - I love cooking, I love eating. So I collect recipes and other valuable food information nuggets that help me in the kitchen.

- **Golf** - My favorite sport to play. If you want to master it, you need to study what works and put in the time!
- **Guitar** - I like to strum the six string on a weekly basis. Don't be fooled, I'm still bad, even after 10 years of playing. But as a friend once told me, "it's the best therapy". I concur.
- **Homebrewing** - Me and a couple buddies got heavily involved a few years ago. Unfortunately, it's been a long time since we brewed a batch. I expect that to change once summer rolls around!
- **Housing** - Keep track of any important documents related to your rent, mortgage or insurance.
- **School** - The vast majority of my college files are in this folder. It's like traveling back in time.
- **Settings** - This is where I save any settings files for programs which can be synced between my PC and Macbook, i.e. FileZilla site manager or Klok time tracking.
- **User Manuals** - For products I use frequently, I keep a PDF copy of the user manual handy. This can range from a software purchase to my washer/dryer.
- **Vacations** - I'm the nerd that puts together a spreadsheet to analyze which house to rent. It's in my blood, what can I say!
- **Website Ideas** - This is where I file any "out-there" or passion projects that I know I don't have the time to focus on at the moment. But if you don't write it down, it may escape you forever.

Don't make the mistake of being completely organized in your business, but not your everyday life. Or vice versa.

Bring a balance to the way you better yourself each day.

Utilize Cloud Services

You must take advantage of cloud services to access important client documents and information from anywhere.

Here are some of my favorite tools to organize and manage the gigabytes of data:

Google Calendar - https://www.google.com/calendar/

If you are planning meetings or scheduling blocks of time to work, I'd strongly recommend Google Calendar.

You can create a new calendar for each client, share it with them, or outsource part of the to-do list. And you can setup e-mail notifications so you never forget when you plan in advance.

Google Drive - https://www.google.com/drive/

I dropped Microsoft Word and Excel years ago. I saw the power of cloud computing and decided to go all-in on Google Drive.

They haven't disappointed me since.

Organizing information into a spreadsheet allows your mind to process it deeply and spot trends more easily.

I use spreadsheets for absolutely everything. And I wrote this book using Google Docs. It's wonderful for editing and collaborating with other Gmail users.

Dropbox - https://www.dropbox.com/

There is no better program for file synchronization.

I've been victim of multiple hard-drive crashes where I lost important data. Fun fact, I lost about 3 months of my Master's thesis work because my laptop died in the university lab. It happened in the 5 minutes I escaped to the restroom.

That was the time I said, "never again".

I've been a proponent of backing up to an external drive, but it's really not necessary today with Dropbox.

If you have multiple computers, all your important files will stay in sync when they are in your Dropbox folder. If you only have one computer, your files are backed up on Dropbox's cloud servers.

Do yourself a favor, test it out.

Evernote - https://evernote.com/

I'm going to take a guess that your browser window has 10+ tabs open. At least, that's how I operate each day. Evernote has been the best tool to alleviate this information overload.

Evernote solves this problem by clipping the article into your account, where you can organize by categories. Once there, it's accessible at your convenience, and without an internet connection.

Instead of leaving tabs open, I clip the content to Evernote and focus on the immediately important tasks.

LastPass - https://lastpass.com/

Remembering passwords is impossible. Using weak passwords is risky.

So don't do either, and choose a password manager like LastPass.

You get a "master password" which you must remember. I like to store this in a text document within my Dropbox folder. So I really don't remember that either, but I know I won't lose it.

From there, LastPass will automatically fill in your username and password for every saved website. They also generate highly secure passwords for each new account you create.

It is a godsend for both security and saving time logging into multiple personal and client websites every day.

xMarks - http://www.xmarks.com/

This company was purchased by LastPass, and I've been a user for years now to sync my bookmarks across all devices.

I used to bookmark everything. Now I bookmark great services/websites and use Evernote for specific articles and research.

Wave Accounting - https://www.waveapps.com/

With the offline component to my business (promotional products), I had to switch to QuickBooks.

But before I made that leap, I used Wave Accounting for all web design work. It's a wonderfully designed and easy to use online accounting service.

Even better, it is free.

Take the Reigns

When someone is paying you, it can be instinctive to do anything they tell you. This is where your business skills need to kick in.

Remember, under the terms of your deal, you are the expert.

This doesn't mean you shouldn't collaborate. In fact, the best result always comes from effortless collaboration between you and the small business owner. Two brains are better than one, and if you can focus that creative energy, magic will happen.

That said, there are always clients who take advantage of you.

They may not be bad people. They are desperate and looking for a solution. It's up to you to set the terms so you can say "no" when they overstep their bounds.

Also, go above and beyond the call of duty.

For instance, I use a project management spreadsheet for each client and I can send them custom reports each month.

If you can analyze the data and suggest improvements, you've put yourself on another level where they will trust you with almost anything online.

It's a process to get there, but the more you take responsibility and come up with new ideas, the quicker you will get to that position.

Download my Google Drive spreadsheet for client project management with the book bonus package:

http://websiteprofitcourse.com/bb/

Chapter 11 - Get Found on Google

Having a website is one thing. Driving traffic to that website is a completely different ballgame.

It's the #1 mistake that beginners make, assuming that customers will find them immediately after the website is launched.

That is simply never the case. It takes time and effort. And it's important to tell a potential client this up front.

However, it's not as difficult as you might think to get found on Google once the website is around for a few months.

This is particularly true with local service businesses.

Let's ponder a situation. Actually I'm not pondering. This happened to me last winter.

I walked into my kitchen, filled the dishwasher with dirty dishes, threw in a detergent tablet and pressed the start button.

I immediately walked out of the kitchen back to my office which isn't very far in my 1-story rancher.

Within a minute, I heard water.

At first, I didn't think anything of it because the dishwasher usually makes sloshing noises, right?

However after 30 seconds, it seemed louder than what I've heard before, so I opened my office door and sprinted back.

What I found was a pipe had frozen and burst, causing water to gush through the recessed lighting in my ceiling, down my walls and out my backdoor.

It took a few minutes to shut off the main water valve and I had to calm down to assess the situation.

My back door was a sheet of ice. It had turned my narrow backyard into a frozen pond because of the gallons of water that flowed down from the pipe in my attic out the door.

Can you guess what the first thing I did was?

I searched Google using the following phrase: plumber in [my city] [my state]

Millions of these searches happen every day. Billions of dollars in revenue are generated from the businesses taking advantage of this search traffic.

And considering the hyper-local nature of this specific keyword phrase, it's much easier to rank your website on Google compared to something more general like "plumbing tips".

Plus, many established local businesses get searches for their company name. Instead of being taken to a 3rd party directory, which may have negative reviews that you cannot control, users will see more trustworthy information on their website.

So how do you get listed on Google?

Method #1 - Pay for Instant Traffic

Here is the fast and easy method:

- Give them your credit card.
- Select keywords to trigger your ad
- Select the price you want to pay for each click to your website
- Once setup, you immediately are put into an auction-style system
- When someone searches, your ad enters the auction with other advertisers
- If your bid per click is enough, your ad will show up, otherwise it will not
- You only pay when someone clicks an ad, not when they appear
- The cost for each click can range from $0.50 to $50.00, depending on the competition and perceived value of the search keyword

This is the Google AdWords program, and it accounts for roughly 90-95% of the money Google makes each year.

It works for one reason, they only show the best ads which are most relevant to the user. Meaning if your ad doesn't perform well, you either pay a premium for each click or you lose the auction and your ad will not appear at all.

On the flip side, if you have an amazingly crafted ad that entices users to click, and it's well matched with the offer on your website, you will pay a reduced price resulting in more traffic for less money.

In my experience with Google AdWords, you pay a higher price when you first open your account.

Over time as the account ages and you test various ads/offers to see what works best, you'll reduce your cost-per-click (CPC). You need to be prepared to lose money or break even in the beginning while you collect data.

Like anything else, it's a learned skill. But if you are willing to test, there are local clients that will pay you to manage their campaigns.

I've personally managed about $35K - $40K in ad spend with just a handful of small business owners in the past couple years. Not massive numbers, but if you get these offline folks new business from people finding them via Google, they will believe in your ability to make things happen.

Method #2 - SEO + Content Marketing

Google aims to show you the absolute most relevant result when you search. That's how they built their fortune.

Those results they show you consist of paid listings as described above and organic listings. Unlike CPC advertising where you pay to play, organic traffic is free and earned over time.

You have to prove to Google that your website is worthing of showing up for certain keywords. Once you do, they will send you traffic naturally when people are searching.

It's impossible to teach the nuances of search engine optimization (SEO) in a few pages, but here's what I've learned that will give you a broad perspective of how the process works:

Google Crawler

SEO starts with this little automated "robot" called the Google Crawler. Its job is to look around the web, jumping from link to link and domain to domain, analyzing the content on each web page.

When it finds a new web page, it "indexes" this information into Google's search database.

Over time, it will come to the same web page and see how often it's updated. If it finds that the content is the same on every visit, it will come less frequently. However if you keep the website fresh, it'll visit more often to see what's new.

This is done on a page-by-page basis. And it's why big sites get articles published on Google faster than you.

Google's index is massive, and you can get a feel for how many competitors there are for every keyword search you perform.

As an example, I just typed in "small business web design" and Google informs me that there are "About 508,000,000 results".

Not an easy task to get to #1 for that term.

Sleazy SEO companies will sell packages to "get your website listed on Google" for $199 or more. Sounds like a reasonable deal, doesn't it?

Well, there is a lot of vagueness with getting listed on Google and what that actually means.

Some people will simply submit your URL to index your website on Google. But as explained previously, Google's crawlers will do this for you for free. Even faster if you link to your website from a larger social website like Twitter or LinkedIn.

It only takes a matter of a couple days to a couple weeks after you register the domain and setup your WordPress website for it to appear in Google's index organically.

Other SEO companies will guarantee #1 rankings. This is when red flags should immediately go up.

Generally these guarantees come with a major stipulation - they will choose keywords that are obscure or have no traffic.

What good is ranking #1 for "best 20 year old saxophonist in williamsburg va"?

You can proudly admire it, but no one else will see it because no one is searching for that phrase.

And no one on earth can guarantee search rankings because it's determined by Google's algorithm.

The only way to assure you're #1 is by paying with CPC traffic. And even then Google can push you down if the offer isn't relevant enough.

Keyword Relevance

Google is both really smart and a little thick-headed.

The sophistication within their search algorithm is almost incomprehensible. It has been refined for 17 years, and has been through major updates along the way, neatly highlighted by MOZ at the URL below:

http://moz.com/google-algorithm-change

But it cannot assume your website topic if you don't provide enough information. You need to explicitly indicate - on several levels - the topic of every page, and how it fits into the overall theme of your website. This means text, photos, filenames, captions, titles, headlines, links, etc.

At the core, you are going to get found by people searching for something really specific - a product, a service or information.

You need to understand your ideal customer and their mindset to uncover the target list of keywords for your website.

The best tool to uncover great keywords to generate content around is the Google Keyword Planner, URL below:

https://adwords.google.com/ko/KeywordPlanner/Home

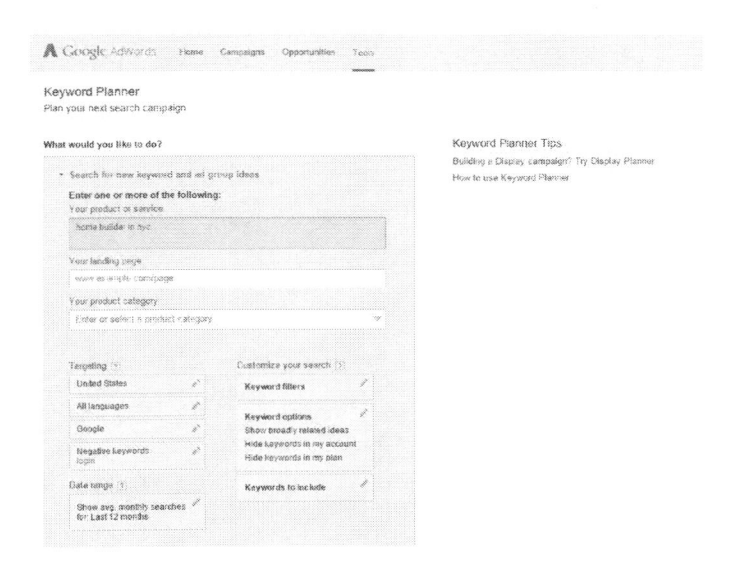

By testing out different ideas, you'll uncover variations you probably never considered. Then you can add those terms throughout your website in a natural way and use as a basis for new content.

Search Rankings

Once Google finds your site, they start to compare it against the other websites in their index.

At first, you won't get any search traffic. That's the sad truth.

But over the next couple months, Google will start to push you higher up the chain if you continue to produce great content on your website and successfully promote it on other platforms.

The more you write, the better the chance someone will find you.

Your first visitors from Google will be searching for ultra-specific and obscure terms. For example "small lightweight and portable hario ceramic coffee mill".

These are called "long-tail" keywords. You cannot predict the exact search, but if you have a lot of resources on a specific topic, you begin to align with some of these searches.

You should want to rank for a couple well-thought out long-tail keywords at the beginning. Use the Google Keyword Planner to see if they get at least a couple hundred searches each month.

Remember, your site doesn't have enough authority to go after competitive keywords from day one.

But there are millions of these long-tail searches each day and that's where you'll develop your first trickle of organic traffic.

In order to get traffic on Google, you must be ranked on the first page.

So if there are 500 million competing web pages for a keyword, you must be in the top 10 to gain any traction at all.

Preferably in the top 5, because people don't scroll to the bottom the majority of the time.

It is a daunting task, but the more you follow a routine with creating and re-purposing content, the easier everything becomes. The more specific your topic for each page/post, the less competition.

You have to take the patient approach when it comes to ranking with keyword relevance on Google. Building authority across your domain takes time and consistent effort.

On-Page SEO

Using keywords wisely within the article is the first step. Then you need to understand how to load the rest of the page with hints to Google that reinforce your page topic.

This, in a nutshell, is on-page SEO.

Here's what you need to focus on:

- **HTML Title** - Put your main keyword first, add descriptive text next. Don't keyword spam. Make the title unique on each page. Target a broader topic on the homepage, and use the specific pages/posts for long-tail keywords. If the website is local, append the city and state name or abbreviation.

- **HTML Meta Description** -By default, this is what Google uses as the description to show when your website appears for a search. If it's persuasive and keyword rich, you'll do better with both ranking and click-through. It's worth noting that Google may display content relevant to the users search instead - it's 100% dependent upon the search intent and Google's algorithm.
- **SEO-Friendly URL** - Don't create several folders or levels to your URL. Make it simple and use your main keyword. I like to change this as one of the first steps after installing WordPress. Within the permalink settings, select post name only to keep it short and sweet, i.e. http://yourwebsite.com/post-name
- **Adding Keywords to Content** - This means be keyword specific in the first paragraph or two to set the tone. Write long posts so there are more search combinations for people to find you. If you have images, use the HTML alt tag and include keywords there. If you embed a YouTube video, make that video centered around the same keywords. Place keywords within HTML heading tags (h1, h2, h3, etc.). But most importantly, do it naturally. Spammy may work today, but it never lasts. Try to weave keywords into a real story.
- **Page Load Speed** - Check out Pingdom Tools or Google's Page Speed Insights, both in the resources section. This is a ranking factor that Google has publicly acknowledged, and there are a bunch of easy fixes. Some of the main culprits are

117

non-optimized JPG images (use save-for-web on Photoshop/Illustrator) and too many external requests.
- **Social Sharing** - You want to make it as easy as possible for people to share the website content. Use a tool like SumoMe which adds social share buttons to every page on your website, with all the most popular services.
- **Internal Links** - Have you ever looked something up on Wikipedia, and then two hours later thought, "Why am I looking at Magnetoception and Cuddle Parties?" Those abundance of links help you stay on Wikipedia longer, sometimes going down the rabbit hole. You can use the same internal linking strategy with your website once you build a library of content. Encourage your clients to participate in the creation of blog posts, photos or videos so it's more authentic.
- **Utilize the Homepage** - This is your highest ranking page. If you want people to visit a specific page on your website, make it a featured link on the homepage. If it's an image link, that will draw more attention.

There are plenty more ins-and-outs with on-page SEO, but this should give you a headstart when you create a website for a local client.

Link Building

The last section was strictly on-page factors. A logical question would be, what is off-page SEO?

For the most part, it is promoting your website on other websites with an established audience, i.e. link building. It's the most important tactic you can use to boost your rankings in a short period of time.

When an authoritative brand or website on Google vouches for your website by providing an editorial link, you benefit by gaining a slice of that trust. The more you diversify the types and amount of links, the better.

Quality trumps quantity. Strive for links on websites that are a logical fit, such as related blogs, niche directories, or community forums.

This was not always the case. It used to be easier to rank on Google with a lot of bad links. I bought into this nonsense years ago.

I purchased article marketing software, which allowed you to write one article, replace some synonyms to give it a touch of uniqueness, then submit this article to thousands of low-quality article directories.

If you had enough links, this worked for a short period of time and you could profit. There were tiered strategies where you would create unique blogs that link to your website, and blast these blogs with low quality links. This was a way to buffer any spam link building to your main website.

But it was only a matter of time until Google started countering these spammy strategies.

With each link you attempt to add to your website, consider the human element. You don't want to buy links purely for SEO benefit. In fact, that is strictly forbidden according to Google's rules.

Ask yourself, would an actual human reading this page expect to see my link here, and is their audience a right match for my offer?

Automated link building strategies are not a good long term idea. Slow and steady wins the race with SEO, as you gather relevant links and people share your page through social media.

Local Business Factors

Small local businesses have a few different factors that set them apart from other types of websites.

The most important difference is the notion of a "citation", or NAP reference. NAP stands for Name, Address and Phone number - the fingerprint of a brick and mortar business.

Much like link building, the more citations you gather from directories or local websites, the better. But make sure you are consistent with them, because that is a critical factor in local search rankings.

You can read a truly comprehensive local SEO roundup by experts at the link below:

http://moz.com/local-search-ranking-factors

Chapter 12 - Build Your Systems

There are plenty of moving parts in a business. The less you need to think about, the better. You can then use that extra brain power for creativity and making vital decisions, not administrative work.

In order to get to that point, there will be a period of experimenting with your ideal processes.

I can't tell you what will work best for you. But I can tell you how I approach the web design process, and share the information I've curated over the years.

Financial

The financial process can be broken down into the following sequence: **proposal, quote, agreement, invoice, and payment**.

The level of formality is going to depend on who you are dealing with on the other end.

If it's a large business, you may need to send them a formal proposal or quote. The jobs will pay better, but there will be more hoops to jump through to get paid. That is the trade-off.

If it's the owner of a kitchen remodeling contracting business, you can have a casual conversation. I did this the other day, collected a setup charge via check, and will bill him monthly for updates/maintenance.

This meeting took place at his dining room table - that is my kind of office.

For new clients, I always require prepayment of some type. For existing clients, I will do requested work and then send an invoice.

You really don't need anything fancy, the important part is getting details ironed out and making sure all project participants are on the same page.

You can use Microsoft Word or Google Docs templates as a starting point. Or check out Wave Accounting for a free online service.

For getting paid, see Chapter 8 on Pricing Structures and Payments.

Marketing

This will vary based upon your chosen niche, but there are rules you can apply to both your client websites and your own.

Content Creation

Generating leads online depends on getting traffic to your website. It shouldn't be a surprise that the websites with the best content win that battle, both on Google and social media.

Here's the good thing - very few local businesses make the effort to produce articles or stay active.

Think of an example for a roofing company. People obviously search for terms like "roofing in [my city]" or "best roofer in [my city]".

But what about someone searching for "leaky roof water damage and mold"?

If you build a website with 2-3 articles surrounding this topic, there's a much better chance it will appear on the first page of Google for related keyword phrases.

This scenario contains a potentially high-converting long-tail keyword. You may only get 5-10 of these visitors a year. But if 2 call and need a new roof immediately, your client just got an extra $15-20K in sales.

If you write a couple articles to pair with the website on launch, or even come up with a content creation schedule, you'll be way ahead of the game with your local clients.

Because it's their business, the more they participate, the better. You will find that some clients have no interest in writing or teaching, though. That's where you can add a paid service.

E-mail Marketing

In the online world, there are two platforms that you own - your website and e-mail list.

You can get attention on hundreds of other platforms like Facebook, Instagram and Twitter. However, on those, you must play by their rules.

You create the rules for your website and communication with e-mail subscribers.

Plus, learning e-mail marketing will allow you to add a new service and increase your income potential.

As you may be noticing, there is a lot of crossover between promoting your own websites and promoting a client website.

I recommend starting with a client website, because they already have an established business and will pay you.

You shouldn't neglect a personal website, though. Even if it's a passion project. It's good to have a long-term idea that you continue to work on and improve. I neglected this for too long.

Sales

I'm no master in sales. I can tell you that for sure. Asking for money is still uncomfortable, even though I know when to do it nowadays.

What has helped me the most is coming up with two documents - a script and FAQ list.

A big part of the sales process is asking questions. A potential client is feeling you out and how you operate, while you want them to divulge details of their business to highlight on the website.

Over time, you begin to hear common questions and you can formulate a better response once you spot these "pain points".

With a full list of questions and common rebuttals, you can fit that into a script to use if you decide to venture into the world of cold calls.

I think it's useful to build a script even if you don't make cold calls. It's a way to refine your communication with every new client.

Training

In the beginning, I thought it would be catchy to tell potential clients, "I can build you a website that you can update yourself."

Not many responded to that message. Small business owners don't want to learn something they don't care about. You are the WordPress expert, not them.

I decided to shift my approach, more along the lines of, "I will build you a professional website that you don't need to touch, text me photos, I'll handle updates. Any problems? Call me."

My ideal clients like this method. Your ideal niche may be the personality types who want to learn WordPress.

In either instance, document how you build a website in as fine detail as possible. Use a Google Spreadsheet to make the process list.

That way, if you ever do need to train a client, you'll be more prepared. And if you don't, you'll be able to train an outsourced worker.

The key point is that you need to eliminate yourself as the limiting factor. Don't spend hours working from ideas in your head. Put those ideas on paper, test them out, and add them to a refined process that you can hand off to someone.

It should be that easy, otherwise you are closer to the freelancer instead of the business owner.

Chapter 13 - Expanding and Growing

I learn something new everyday. And right now there is a thought that is resonating with me.

Sometimes we don't know what our true passion is, yet it can be uncovered through action. This is the central topic of Chris Guillebeau's book, "The Happiness of Pursuit" - which is on my future reading list.

People think it's the other way around where happiness is a destination. But it's not. Happiness comes through daily progress. Don't treat happiness like the top of a mountain you have to achieve or else you'll fall.

You may find yourself on a path you never considered, and you need to be open to the possibilities. The best thing for you may be right around that new corner.

This book is a prime example. I couldn't wait to leave college so I'd never have to write a paper again. I shunned the concept of blogging because I didn't enjoy writing. I thought teaching would never interest me because I only considered it in a classroom setting.

Now, through years of experience, I literally cannot wait to brainstorm new topics and sit down with a cup of coffee to uncover my thoughts on paper.

I've said it before, you cannot predict the future. Just be open to learning and growing as a person, the rest tends to take care of itself.

With a dose of positivity out of the way, you need to be ruthless to grow as a business.

Firing or saying no to bad clients can be the best move you make. This frees your time and energy to grow with better ones who treat you (or your wallet) with more respect.

I define a bad client as those who call when they need something immediately. That's a sign they value their time more than yours. And on a personal level, you should know those people that you don't enjoy communicating with as opposed to the clients where it's a two-way conversation.

Here are actionable steps for you to get more of those great clients after your first paid projects:

Upsell Your Current Clients

Anyone will tell you that the easiest way to increase business is to sell more to your current clients, not finding new ones.

It seems counterintuitive at first, but you have the best relationship with them and you've enticed them past the most important step - handing over payment.

You have to ask yourself, what else would they pay for? What else would actually be of value to their business?

As I mentioned previously, you can add so many services with web design - content creation, e-mail marketing, referral programs, local cross-promotions, online advertising (Google + Facebook), photos, videos, offline services (business cards, shirts), etc.

Don't offer them all at first. Master one at a time until you feel like you have above average skills.

Make sure one client is happy with the outcome of a new service before you push hard for the others to join. Use the first attempt as a way to document your own process and become more efficient so you can earn more money per hour the next implementation.

Ask For Referrals

Referrals are the best way to get new business. They cost no money, and they are a virtual guaranteed customer.

Your best clients will refer you anytime they think you can help someone, but other clients might need an extra push.

The first step is asking. Send an e-mail or call them to see if they know anyone to put you in touch with.

You can even create a referral program with an incentive for them to bring you new business.

Creative Google Search

If you are looking for business opportunities outside of your current client base, why not start with Google?

Even if a small business doesn't have a website, chances are their contact information (phone or address) is located on a directory somewhere.

Determine the types of businesses you want to work with, and start searching!

Keep in mind, for all the search ideas I give below, you can be as specific or broad as you like. Search for business type only, within the entire state, your city only, etc.

Find Old Websites

Most websites have a tagline at the bottom which includes the copyright statement and year.

Use this to your advantage by searching Google for old websites in your neighborhood or state that need an upgraded online presence.

Below are some search phrases to uncover gems:

- "copyright 2000..2013" [city] [state] [business type]
- "2000..2013 copyright" [city] [state] [business type]
- "2000..2013 all rights reserved" [city] [state] [business type]
- "all rights reserved 2000..2013" [city] [state] [business type]

Find Other Platforms

If you see a local website built by a large service like Web.com or SuperMedia, it never hurts to contact the business and see if they are happy with their experience.

One of my clients stopped using the big guys because he said every time he spoke on the phone, it was a new customer service rep who didn't understand his website at all.

See if you can get a local business to convert to you. Here are some searches:

- "web page design by web.com" [city] [state] [business type]
- "website powered by network solutions" [city] [state] [business type]
- "homestead make a website for your business" [city] [state] [business type]
- "designed by * using intuit" [city] [state] [business type]
- "using intuit website templates" [city] [state] [business type]
- "powered by supermedia, llc" [city] [state] [business type]
- "this website was created using 1&1 mywebsite" [city] [state] [business type]
- "2005..2014 hibu,inc. all rights reserved" [city] [state] [business type]
- "website provided by vistaprint" [city] [state] [business type]
- "yellow book usa, inc. all rights reserved" [city] [state] [business type]

Use Directories

Here's where you can find the businesses that don't have a website. If they've been in business for a couple years, they are likely listed in one of the major directories.

You can browse each directory manually, or search using Google's site operator:

- site:manta.com [city] [state] [business type]
- site:superpages.com [city] [state] [business type]
- site:angieslist.com [city] [state] [business type]
- site:yelp.com [city] [state] [business type]

Blog Your Experiences

I waited way too long to do this. Writing is so good for your thought process, your creativity and your ability to sell - for both you and your clients.

Even if it's bi-weekly, pick a schedule to write about a topic you are passionate about, then stick with it.

Going back to the "Content Creation" section in the last chapter, you can blog about your experiences setting up your first couple client websites.

It has a handful of benefits besides the inner ones mentioned above.

First, you'll begin to see search traffic coming to your website, especially if you do a little keyword research to uncover low competition phrases. This can take a couple months, but will happen if you are focused on one topic and consistent.

Second, the people who do find you will have a much better concept of who you are as a person and your methods.

The biggest concern a lot of us have when publishing our knowledge is that others will steal the ideas and get credit for them. You'll feel like you missed out.

In reality, this doesn't happen often. At least not as much as you would think. It's because people have their own obligations. They don't have enough free time to take an idea they never considered, and implement it.

You'll build a much higher level of trust and more of your website visitors will take the next step to contact you.

Sell Previous Results

Telling a potential client you can build them a website is not a strong enough hook anymore.

I can tell you from my experience working with business owners, you receive weekly e-mails from random people regarding web and graphic services. You become immune to generic pitches.

A better strategy is relating to your prospect by saying, "I've worked with a couple similar businesses to yours and we're seeing 10 extra calls each month from Google." You are coming to them with a more intriguing offer.

That's why it's important to do work up front before you charge the big bucks.

You don't need to drive enormous traffic numbers. Take your best result and spin it into a spicy headline.

For instance, if you have a client ranked for a local keyword you can mention, "The website we created is listed high on Google when people search locally. It's not a flood of traffic but it's extremely targeted when they find our client." You're being honest and emphasizing the best possible outcome.

Or if you don't have specific numbers, be more generic by saying, "One of our client's had no idea how many visitors their website received before. Now we are tracking that information and sending a report each month so we can make smarter decisions moving forward." This is easy with Google Analytics.

You want to highlight that a website is more than digital files, it's a business asset that pays for itself time-and-time again when utilized correctly.

It should be the hub for all online and offline marketing campaigns.

Outsource or Partner

Some of us are strong with code, some with design, some with project management, some with communication.

In the beginning, it's important to handle everything to get a perspective of the holistic process of website creation and on-going maintenance.

But there does come a point of diminishing returns, where your time is best spent focusing on bigger picture ideas.

In order to do this, you need to have a process and either outsource tasks or partner with someone to handle a large chunk of the project.

A great example of a partnership is a graphic design agency with a web development agency. Individually, they have their own employees and processes, but they collaborate effectively on a large client website.

You can take this same philosophy, but on a one-to-one level with a designer and a coder.

Personally, I think it's best to start small when it comes to outsourcing. You don't want to partner with someone who may be unreliable. Instead, give them small tasks and once they build up trust with you, offer larger projects.

I'm guilty of spreading myself too thin at times. But I have successfully outsourced design and writing. And it's a great feeling to get a finished product without working on it!

When outsourcing, make sure you provide a checklist of what needs to be done, otherwise expect mistakes. Teach your process more accurately by using screencast tutorials, so others can imitate your steps.

Get Started Today

If you made it this far, I can't help but sincerely thank you again for finishing!

I hope this book has provided a couple "aha" moments and resources that you can take action on today.

I'll end with how I started - working with websites is challenging and fun.

When you experience small wins, you'll know there is nothing stopping you from moving forward.

That mindset is half the battle, regardless of your level of expertise. It has to be given how quickly technology changes.

Over time you develop a better decision making process with every angle of online marketing.

I can't stress it enough, you must do something each day to move forward. If you take a week off at the beginning, you'll lose momentum and give up.

That's why I recommend maintaining a personal website, even if it's not tech-related. You can test new techniques there without repercussions. It's also an ideal avenue to hone your writing skills, something I omitted for years.

As my first extended writing, I know I have a lot to improve.

I also had a lot of fun recounting stories and sharing the broad knowledge that I've accumulated through years of experience with personal and client websites.

Please check out my blog for more how-to articles and video tutorials on building client websites with WordPress:

http://websiteprofitcourse.com/

And you can download all the FREE extras with my book bonus package at the link below:

http://websiteprofitcourse.com/bb/

List of Resources

Here is a list of my most used resources that I've collected over the past 5+ years. You can rest assured they are all top notch books, services, and tools.

Books

Choose Yourself by James Altucher – As a board member of a job recruiting company, he spells out what he sees in the near future. And it's less full-time employees and more people utilizing their unique skills to work for themselves. Some great tips include write 10 ideas a day, give them away for free, offer a service, build connections, be grateful for what you have. If you develop this practice, success and money will be a byproduct.

How I Lost 170 Million Dollars: My Time as #30 at Facebook by Noah Kagan – An interesting look at the early days of Facebook. Also a tale of the mindset it takes to recover from bitter disappointment. Short read, and I thoroughly enjoyed it.

Quantum Golf: The Path to Golf Mastery by Kjell Enhager – This is like "The Greatest Salesman in the World" for golf. One or two techniques, but mostly it's the mindset you need to succeed on the course. And having played for 10+ years with a ton of people, I can say that most folks have a harder time dealing with their own thoughts than they do with their swing. That's why I love golf, it's an incredibly humbling sport (look at Tiger

Woods). You will learn several lasting lessons that apply to other areas of your life.

Steal Like an Artist: 10 Things Nobody Told You About Being Creative by Austin Kleon – All creative people are simply inspired by others. They take pieces of art they connect with, then re-purpose in their own way. He provides examples and offers ways to become more creative yourself. One of my favorite is separating your computer desk from your creative space, which should have colors, papers, tape, scissors, etc. It takes you back to being a kid and it absolutely works!

The 4-Hour Workweek by Tim Ferriss – The title has ignited debates among business folks. However, the end-goal is not to work 4 hours a week – it's to increase your per hour output. And he provides a roadmap of several ways to do just that, whether you are an entrepreneur or want to advance your career.

The E-Myth Revisited by Michael E. Gerber – This was the first book that really taught me the difference between working IN your business and working ON your business. If you are doing tasks everyday that can be outsourced for $20/hr, you are not using your time wisely. It also reminds me of a common question by Kevin O'Leary on Shark Tank, "if you got hit by a bus, how would I make my money back?" Harsh, yes. But if your business dies with you, you haven't set up the right systems as a business owner.

The Greatest Salesman in the World by OG Mandino – I read this in a day while camping, and it's one of the most concise and well written stories about what it takes to succeed as either a salesman or entrepreneur. It wasn't exactly what I expected, but it's one of those books that teaches you mindset over technique. It won me over.

Business

MailChimp – E-mail marketing tool with a free option to kick-start your communication with leads and clients

Wave Accounting - Easy to use, great looking, and free, which is just what you need when you only have a couple projects to invoice

Color Scheme

Color Combos – Browse a variety of color combinations that may inspire your design

Color Scheme Designer – Generates color palettes based on 1-color

Colour Lovers – Community of people who share colors, palettes and patterns

Hex to RGB Converter – Use this tool to get the correct color code for your stylesheet

Copywriting

Spell Checker – Find typos on any page on your website using this tool

CSS

CSS Media Queries – Use within your custom CSS to make your website responsive

CSS Stats – Find out the most used CSS properties on your (or any) website

CSS Tricks – Popular Blog with CSS Tutorials on New Features and Common Issues

Skeleton Responsive CSS Framework – Use their column-based grid layout to quickly develop your HTML/CSS website

W3 Schools CSS Tutorials – Learn the Basics of CSS with Examples

Domain Registration

GoDaddy – Register and Manage Your Domains

Fonts

1001 Free Fonts – Many Free Fonts to Download

FontSpring – Worry-Free Font Licensing for All Devices

Font Squirrel – Free & Premium Fonts

Google Fonts – Free Fonts to Download or Easily Embed on Your Website

MyFonts – Premium Font Licensing

TypeKit – Font Service that Allows You to Use Thousands of Fonts on Your Projects

Google Chrome Browser Add-Ons

ColorZilla – Pick Out Colors from a Website

Dimensions – Determine the Pixel Width or Height of Elements on a Website

Evernote Web Clipper – Clips Content from the Web into Your Evernote Account

Google Dictionary – Provides a Definition for Every Word You Double-Click to Highlight

LastPass – Password Manager that Generates and Stores Secure Passwords for All Your Website Accounts

Link Checker – Checks for Broken Links Automatically on Any Web Page

PageRank Checker – Determines Google PageRank (0 to 10) of Any Web Page

Wappalyzer – Find Out the Technology Behind Every Website You Visit

XMarks – Sync Your Bookmarks Between Browsers and Computers

HTML

HTML Sandbox – Split Window to Simultaneously Test Your HTML Code and View Results

W3 Schools HTML Tutorials – Learn the Basics of HTML with Examples

Images

PlaceHold.it – Don't have images just yet? Use this to generate placeholders

UnSplash – Use the free, high-resolution stock images for anything you want (seriously)

jQuery

jQuery – Javascript Library for Really Cool Animations and Easy-to-Install Features

jQuery API – Help for All Functions Included in the jQuery Library

jQuery UI – More Animations/Widgets Built on jQuery like Drag-n-Drop, Accordion Menu, Progress Bar, Date Picker from a Calendar

Measurement & Tracking

Google Analytics – Analyze your website traffic and make smarter decisions based on actual data

Optimizely – Easy A/B experiments on your website to test variations on colors, buttons and copy

BuiltWith Trends – See the current trends in web technologies that are being used by websites across the internet

Productivity & Efficiency

Dropbox – Sync Files Between All Your Devices

Evernote – Collect, Save and Search Your Notes Easily

FileZilla – Transfer Files from Your Computer to Web Host with FTP, Sync Settings via Dropbox

Klok – Track How Long You Spend on Projects, Sync Settings via Dropbox

Notepad++ – Powerful text editor that applies styles to different code such as HTML, CSS and Javascript

Q/A + Forums

Quora – Question and answer site with authority contributors like CEOs, entrepreneurs and other influential people

StackOverflow – Code-Centric Q/A Website

SEO

SerpFox – Easy-to-use tool to record your Google rankings over time for multiple keywords and phrases, plus export capability

Local Search Ranking Factors – Detailed post regarding the trends in local SEO by a round-up of experts

Social Media & Sharing

Buffer App – Schedule your social media posts in advanced

Embed.ly – Easily embed content from other sources or make it easy for your audience to share your posts

SumoMe – Website plugin that adds responsive social sharing buttons to every page of your website (plus other AMAZING features)

Topsy – Social media analytics tool

Testing Tools

301 Redirect Checker – Tool to ensure a URL redirects to the correct page

Google Page Speed Insights – Quick Test with Advice on How to Improve Your Website Speed

iPad Peek – Virtually Shows How Your Website Looks on an iPad & iPhone

MX Toolbox – Test the DNS/MX Settings of Your Domain and Web Hosting

Pingdom Page Speed – Test the Performance & Speed of Each Page on Your Website

Viewport Resizer – Responsive Web Design Bookmarklet that Allows You to Dynamically Resize Your Browser Window

Textures & Patterns

Pattern Cooler – Pick from Several Repeating Patterns and Customize Colors

Subtle Patterns – Repeating Patterns Great for Website Background

Texture King – Free Stock Textures Ranging from Grunge to Concrete and more

Vectors & Graphics

All Free Download – Free vectors and other graphics

Vecteezy – Free vector art to use in your designs

Website Hosting

HostGator – Single and Multi-Website Hosting Plans to Start Your Web Design Business

WordPress

WordPress.org – Self-Hosted WordPress Installation

WordPress Documentation – Information on WordPress Theme Structure and Back-End Code

WordPress Plugins – Extend the Functionality of Your Website with Popular Plugins

WordPress Theme – Free & Responsive – A Modern and Professional Looking WordPress Theme at No Cost

WordPress Plugins – My Favorites

Advanced Automatic Updates – Automatically updates your WordPress core software, including plugins and themes

Ajax Event Calendar – Easy to use and slick calendar of events with links to Google Maps

Akismet – Comment spam blocker which is normally pre-installed with WordPress

BackupBuddy – Easy-to-use automatic backup software which works with services like Dropbox, Amazon S3 and others

Better WordPress Minify – Combine several CSS and Javascript files into one to save load time

Contact Form 7 – Build contact forms and surveys which can be added to any page on your website

Disqus – Advanced comment system which is used in place of the standard comments with WordPress

Google XML Sitemaps – Provide a list of every URL on your website so people can find you on Google

Growmap Anti Spambot – Adds a checkbox to the comment form for users to confirm they are human

iThemes Plugin Suite – Great pack of premium plugins that includes everything from BackupBuddy to photo galleries

Limit Login Attempts – As the name suggests, it increases security by blocking anyone that tries to login too many times

Responsive Lightbox – Add the image "lightbox" effect using a variety of different services

Search and Replace – Search and replace text within your WordPress database instead of manually updating several entries

SEO by Yoast – The best plugin to help your website content achieve #1 rankings in Google

Simple 301 Redirects – Redirect one URL to another

SumoMe – Website plugin that adds responsive social sharing buttons to every page of your website (plus other AMAZING features)

TablePress – Insert a database or table within one of your posts/pages

User Role Editor – Change what different user levels are allowed to update on your website

W3 Total Cache – Caching plugin that helps your website to load faster, best for VPS or dedicated hosting

WP Super Cache – Caching plugin that helps your website to load faster, best for shared hosting

Made in the USA
Columbia, SC
30 August 2019